Through the
FRENCH
CANALS

Through the FRENCH CANALS

Philip Bristow

fifth edition

MACMILLAN LONDON

First published 1970 in Great Britain by
Navigator Publishing Limited

2nd edition 1972, 3rd edition 1975, 4th edition 1979

This edition published 1982 by
NAUTICAL BOOKS
An imprint of Macmillan London Limited
4 Little Essex Street
London WC2R 3LF
Reprinted 1984

Associated companies throughout the world

Filmset in Great Britain by
BAS Printers Limited, Over Wallop, Hampshire
Printed in Hong Kong

British Library Cataloguing in Publication Data
Bristow, Philip
    Through the French canals.—5th ed.
    1. Inland navigation—France
    2. Boats and boating—France
    I. Title.
    797.1   GV835.3.F/

    ISBN 0-333-32927-9

Despite every effort to ensure that information given in this book is accurate and up to date, it is regretted that neither author nor publisher can accept responsibility for errors or omissions.

To Emma

perfect companion of many cruises who made this book possible.

Acknowledgements

I am indebted to many Departments of the French Government for the facts and figures that they have kindly made available to me; to the many offices of the *Syndicat d'Initiative* who have patiently dealt with my considerable demands upon their time; and particularly to Georges Normand, *Chargé de Mission, Commissariat Général au Tourisme*, 8 Avenue de l'Opera, Paris, for his kindness and help.

Note: Depths of water are shown throughout in metres, including all harbour plans.

Contents

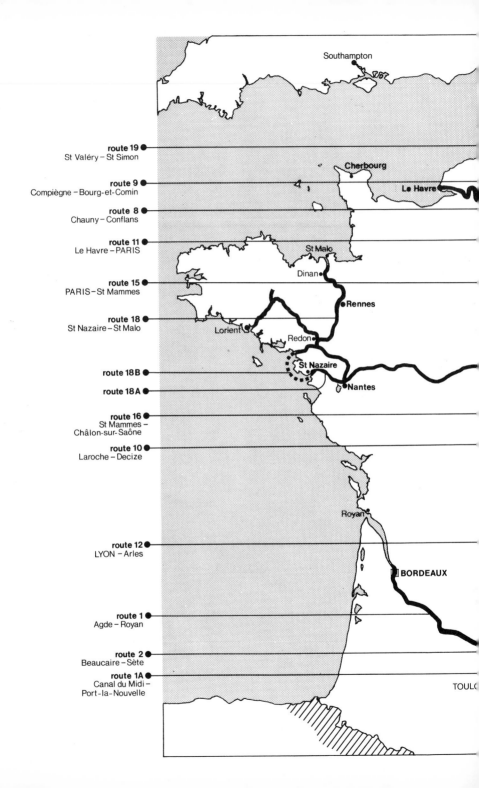

Southampton

route 19 ●
St Valéry – St Simon

Cherbourg

route 9 ●
Compiègne – Bourg-et-Comin

Le Havre

route 8 ●
Chauny – Conflans

route 11 ●
Le Havre – PARIS

St Malo

route 15 ●
PARIS – St Mammes

Dinan ●

route 18 ●
St Nazaire – St Malo

● **Rennes**

Lorient ●

Redon ●

route 18 B ●

St Nazaire

route 18 A ●

● **Nantes**

route 16 ●
St Mammes –
Châlon-sur-Saône

route 10 ●
Laroche – Decize

Royan ●

route 12 ●
LYON – Arles

■ **BORDEAUX**

route 1 ●
Agde – Royan

route 2 ●
Beaucaire – Sète

route 1A ●
Canal du Midi –
Port-la-Nouvelle

TOUL

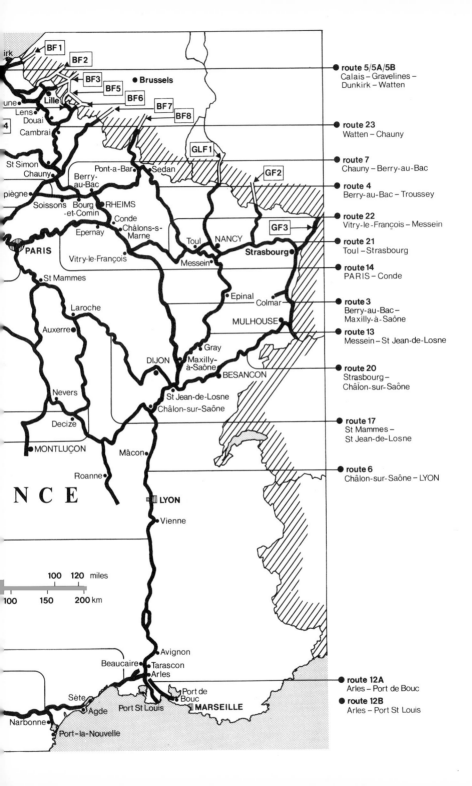

route 5/5A/5B
Calais – Gravelines –
Dunkirk – Watten

route 23
Watten – Chauny

route 7
Chauny – Berry-au-Bac

route 4
Berry-au-Bac – Troussey

route 22
Vitry-le-François – Messein

route 21
Toul – Strasbourg

route 14
PARIS – Conde

route 3
Berry-au-Bac –
Maxilly-à-Saône

route 13 Messein – St Jean-de-Losne

route 20
Strasbourg –
Châlon-sur-Saône

route 17
St Mammes –
St Jean-de-Losne

route 6
Châlon-sur-Saône – LYON

route 12A
Arles – Port de Bouc

route 12B
Arles – Port St Louis

List of Illustrations

Maps

Introduction

by
GEORGES NORMAND
Chargé de Mission

COMMISSARIAT GENERAL   8 avenue de l'Opéra,
AU TOURISME   PARIS

How to travel in France

I am pleased to have this opportunity to write the introduction to Philip Bristow's new book, because my interest for the last two years has been to tell everyone about the rivers and canals of France. Why? Because I discovered that a good Frenchman like myself knew nothing about waterways in my own country. My belated discovery was that they were by far the most beautiful in Europe and, at the same time, one could travel around almost all of France by boat.

I also found that other countries were utilizing waterways for tourism in a way we were not.

What is tourism? What did it mean a few years ago? Tourism meant that a certain class had the time, the money, to go to the Riviera. That was the European rendezvous of those days. We have come far from this conception in the last ten years. So far, that I think we should use a new word.

Leisure (*loisir* in French) is a new concept that needs our attention. These days, leisure is available to everyone who has a regular job with a vacation. Leisure is now the privilege of all classes. And everyone can find appropriate ways of using their *loisir*.

Most people in our twentieth century are used to classical vacations. Here are some classical examples:

A tour of Europe as well as a tour of the United States. The main capitals or main cities. This is tiring, but interesting, and should be done at least once.

A summer or winter resort, where you spend your full time bathing or skiing, with a heavy social life at night.

Holidays at your own country house, one that has been in the family for years or that you have just bought. This is also nice.

Motoring on super-highways or byways. This offers surprises with lots of charm, except that the driver must look only ahead and cannot see the country. His wife does not dare to look to the side either. They must find a room for the night, or if they camp it could rain—and camping in the rain!

Another way is with your own caravan. This has its advantages, but there again, you must not go too fast to see the countryside, and the roads are dangerous—more and more dangerous—one wonders what it will be like in the future. Will it be possible to use a car or will it have to be driven automatically, robot-style?

I want to enthusiastically recommend another way of enjoying one's vacation.

Water-roads—off the beaten track, away from the noise of highways, away from the multiple dangers of high-speed driving, away from polluted air, crowds, not the moon, but another land—a land so different from ours, that our conceptions of leisure, our dreams of future vacations will be changed.

The luxury of these days will be a speed limit of 5 knots in a world where you will find peace and repose for the body and soul. A therapeutic treatment like a spa, only you will float on the water, not drink it.

How does one 'travel' on these waterways? Not travel, but float, glide, or ride the canals. By boat, of course. On board you can have a bicycle, camping equipment, to ride the canal roads, find a wild bank, pitch a tent and stay longer. This is an inexpensive and a liberated way to move about. No policeman will stop you for speeding.

If you are more mechanically inclined, you can always take a small boat with an outboard motor, follow the same waterways, you will be asked for nothing or charged nothing as you stop over. This is a free land. On your way you will find some lovely little auberges, where you can have a drink or a good meal, *pas cher*.

Thus we come to a more elaborate way of travelling. Any boat, whose draft is around 1,22m (with an air draft of 3,05m), will carry you all over France (length 35,35m, width 4,72m). You should check your route, as some of the waterways have locks shorter than those dimensions. Some French boat builders have realized, following the example of the United States, that the houseboat is the most convenient on the waterways.

Some captains prefer to be at the wheel of a He boat, one that looks like one. But often, the she partner of a boat prefers to have a She boat—one with comforts such as a fridge, gas oven, shower, and what not. I like comfort myself, and think that houseboats are the most comfortable means to explore the waterways.

If you don't want the responsibility of driving your own boat, one you either own or rent, you can use cruise boats or hotel boats, a most enjoyable way of visiting a country like France. There are charter boats offering full comfort, fine food, nice lodging, plus excursions along the way. The water-roads of France are lovely, restful, and often wild in their own way. Anyone who enjoys nature will profit from every moment of their trip. You can even try your hand at fishing along the way.

But if you are in a hurry, if you seek an exciting life and fashionable resorts, then perhaps you will be bored with the tranquil water-routes. In the year 2000 this supreme luxury might become prohibitive in price. This is the luxury of peace that the canals of France offer you now.

1 Summary of Route Details

ROUTE 9	COMPIEGNE to BOURG-ET-COMIN via Soissons	River Oise, River Aisne
ROUTE 10	LAROCHE to DECIZE via Auxerre, Clameçy	River Yonne, Canal du Nivernais
ROUTE 11	LE HAVRE to PARIS via Rouen, Elbeuf, Vernon, Mantes	River Seine
ROUTE 12	LYON to ARLES via Vienne, Valence, Montélimar, Bollène, Avignon, Tarascon	River Rhône
ROUTE 12A	ARLES to FOS-SUR-MER	Canal d'Arles à Bouc
ROUTE 12B	ARLES to PORT ST. LOUIS	River Rhône
ROUTE 13	MESSEIN to ST. JEAN-DE-LOSNE via Epinal, Gray	Canal de l'Est, River Saône
ROUTE 14	PARIS to CONDE via Joinville, Meaux, Château-Thierry, Epernay, Ay	River Marne
ROUTE 15	PARIS to ST. MAMMES via Melun	River Seine
ROUTE 16	ST. MAMMES to CHALON-SUR-SAONE via Montargis, Briare, Nevers, Decize, Digoin, Montceau-les-Mines, Chagny	Canal du Loing, Canal de Briare, Canal latéral à la Loire, Canal du Centre
ROUTE 17	ST. MAMMES to ST. JEAN-DE-LOSNE via Sens, Joigny, Tonnere, Montbard, Dijon	River Seine, River Yonne, Canal de Bourgogne
ROUTE 18	ST. NAZAIRE to ST. MALO via Nantes, Redon, Rennes, Dinan	River Loire, River Erdre, Canal de Nantes à Brest, River Villaine, Canal d'Ille et Rance, River Rance
ROUTE 19	ST. VALERY to ST. SIMON via Abbeville, Amiens, Peronne	Canal de la Somme
ROUTE 20	STRASBOURG to CHALON-SUR-SAONE via Colmar, Mulhouse, Besançon, Dole	Canal du Rhône au Rhin, River Saône
ROUTE 21	TOUL to STRASBOURG via Nancy	Canal de la Marne au Rhin
ROUTE 22	VITRY-LE-FRANCOIS to MESSEIN via Bar-le-Duc, Toul	Canal de la Marne au Rhin, Canal de l'Est

ROUTE 23	WATTEN to CHAUNY via St. Omer, Bethune, Lille, Cambrai, St. Quentin	River Aa, Canal de Neuffosse, Canal d'Air Canal de la Deule, Ca: de la Sensée, River Esc Canal de Saint-Quent:

From Belgium into France

ROUTE BF/1	FURNES to DUNKIRK	Canal de Nieuwpoort, Canal de Furnes
ROUTE BF/2	MENIN to ARMENTIERES	River Lys
ROUTE BF/3	ESPIERRES to LILLE	Canal de l'Espierres, Canal de Roubaix, Canal de la Deule
ROUTE BF/4	ANTOING to DOUAI	River Escaut, River Scarpe
ROUTE BF/5	ANTOING to CONDE	River Escaut
ROUTE BF/6	BLATON to CONDE	Canal de Pommeroeu Antoing, Canal de Mons à Conde
ROUTE BF/7	CHARLEROI to MAUBEUGE	River Sambre
ROUTE BF/8	NAMUR to PONT-A-BAR	River Meuse

From Germany and Luxembourg into France

ROUTE GLF/1	REMERSCHEN to FROUARD	River Moselle

From Germany into France

ROUTE GF/2	KLEINBLITTERSDORF to GONDREXANGE	River Saar, Canal des Houilleres de la Sarre
ROUTE GF/3	LAUTERBOURG to STRASBOURG	River Rhine

2 Through Routes to the Mediterranean

LE HAVRE to PARIS	369km	7 locks

PARIS to LYON via THE MARNE
Route: River Seine, River Marne,
Canal latéral à la Marne, Canal de
la Marne à la Saône, River Saône   726km   166 locks

PARIS to LYON via BURGUNDY
Route: River Seine to Montereau,
River Yonne to Laroche, Canal de
Bourgogne to St. Jean-de-Losne,
River Saône   636km   *228 locks

PARIS to LYON via THE BOURBONNAIS
Route: River Seine to St. Mammes,
Canal du Loing to Buges, Canal de
Briare to Briare, Canal latéral à la
Loire to Digoin, Canal du Centre to
Châlon-sur-Saône, River Saône   639km   167 locks

*There is a tunnel over two miles long at the summit

3   Stay in the Inland Waterways

On most occasions when the inland waterways of France are mentioned it is in connection with a passage to the Mediterranean, as though the waterways were only to be considered as a route to the sea. It is a pity that the Mediterranean casts such a spell, for that part of it within range of a limited time cruise, has very little to offer the small boat owner compared with the peace and interest of the French canals.

Just as mountaineers have ambitions to get to the top of mountains so, it appears, do yachtsmen have ambitions to get to the Mediterranean; having achieved his ambition the mountaineer simply returns. For the yachtsman the return is somewhat more involved, although a yacht with sufficient power can now get back up the Rhône (of which more later). The knowledge and experience needed to get back via Biscay and St. Malo is far greater than that needed for a cruise in the canals.

The Mediterranean has a great deal to offer the yachtsman with time to get far away from the crowded anchorages and harbours; or even for the man who can afford to base his boat there. But for the more usual limited time cruise, the time available would be far better spent exploring the inland waterways.

For instance, cruising in the Mediterranean you obviously have to seek a harbour when you want to stop. You have to find one, enter, look for a spot to tie up. You will be lucky indeed if this spot happens to be clean, quiet, handy for getting ashore, near to shops; you will put up with these disadvantages rather than face the upheaval of going out again to seek another harbour that may be no better. In the canals you can stop practically where you like at any time.

The attractive harbours that you can reach within your time allowance will be packed with other yachts. With the possible exception of the new Languedoc-Roussillon development, the attractive and fashionable Mediterranean harbours have waiting lists for *permanent* moorings stretching into the years ahead; visiting yachtsmen simply cannot be accommodated, except perhaps for a night stop after which a heavy charge is levied to ensure that visiting boats are kept on the move (and even this is not always possible in the peak holiday periods). Attractive canal stops are seldom crowded.

You will have no choice but to go into many unattractive harbours. It is easy to forget, when thinking of the Mediterranean, that there is industry there, too. It will be a rare occasion indeed that you will need to stop in an unattractive place in the inland waterways.

Days spent cruising at sea are often a bore; in a sailing yacht the unpredictability of the wind is an irritation as well. Whether sailing or motor cruising it is easy to sympathize with the songwriter who wrote: 'we went to sea to see the world but all we saw was the sea'. I sympathize with the lady who said that she liked entering harbour and was quite interested in leaving harbour, but found the time in between a complete bore. There is no 'time in between' when you cruise in the inland waterways, for a whole panorama is unfolding at every moment—woods, towns, fields, little villages where you can step ashore to shop and explore.

At sea your progress is determined by weather; winds suddenly appear, frequently with strengths of up to Force 6, dying away to leave complete calm. Weather never interferes with your inland waterway progress (except at more or less predictable times of drought and flood).

Waves knock you about at sea, particularly in the Mediterranean where they arrive violently and unexpectedly. In harbours the ships and fishing fleets churn up waves without consideration for the yachtsmen's slumbers. There are no waves in the waterways; the wash from passing craft is less than that in harbours, and on most of the waterways no traffic moves at night.

Harbours cost money, in fact the attractive harbours are alarmingly expensive (if you can get in for a brief stay at all); the inland waterways cost nothing.

Down the Rhône from Lyon to the Mediterranean is around 320km, a two to three day journey (although the powerful barges do it in half this time). As I explain in a later chapter the business of cruising down the Rhône has been much simplified in recent years and, indeed, the business of cruising *UP* the Rhône has been made possible for a great many craft. The engagement of a pilot is not compulsory nor really necessary but they are available if needed.

The expedition down the Rhône to 'see the sea' can use up time and effort and money which might be more profitably spent in the canals if one is on a limited time cruise. In fact the sad thing is that people with just time to spare to explore the French canals do not do so because they do not have the time to get to the Mediterranean and back. Obviously, in thinking only in terms of getting to the Mediterranean, the very time involved rules out a cruise in the French canals for most people.

Consider, instead, a planned cruise through France. The **Route Map** (see pages 8–9), and the **Route Details Section** at the end of the book, shows the main navigable waterways of France arranged as 23 routes, connecting from one waterway junction to another. The towns and villages on, or near, each of these routes are also set out in detail in this section. Distances and the number of locks are shown.

For instance, if you plan to enter France at Le Havre, Route 11 will describe the route as far as Paris. If you wish to turn off before Paris, you can do so at Conflans-St. Honorine (Route 8), up, say, to Compiègne, branching right on Route 9 to Bourg-et-Comin, continuing on Route 7 to Berry-au-Bac, turning right on Route 3 as far as Conde-sur-Marne where you may take Route 14 to Paris; then back on Route 11 to return to Le Havre and you will have covered 1071km, passed through 72 locks, and sampled a little champagne on the way, perhaps.

		Km	*Locks*
Route 11	Le Havre to Conflans River Seine	290	6
TURN LEFT			
Route 8	Conflans to Compiègne River Oise	93	7
TURN RIGHT			
Route 9	Compiègne to Bourg-et-Comin River Aisne	64	7
CONTINUE			
Route 7	Bourg-et-Comin to Berry-au-Bac Canal latéral à l'Aisne	21	1

TURN RIGHT

Route 3	Berry-au-Bac to Conde-sur-Marne	58	26
	Canal de l'Aisne à Marne		

TURN RIGHT

Route 14	Conde to Paris	183	15
	River Marne		
Route 11	Paris to Le Havre	362	7
	River Seine		
		1071	72

How long this would take would obviously depend upon the number of hours you wished to spend in cruising every day, but my wife and I would reckon to make it a reasonable three to four weeks' cruise.

Many permutations and combinations of other routes can be planned along these lines; but the main point to be borne in mind is that anyone with even three or four weeks to spare can enjoy a cruise in the French canals. Cruises can be tailor-made to fit in with the time available.

In order to plan what distance you can cruise in the time you have available you would not be far out if you reckoned upon averaging 4 knots between locks and thirty minutes to pass through each lock. (This is simply a rough average for planning purposes only. At some of the bigger locks a wait of several hours is not uncommon.) Some routes have many more locks than others and how many you can manage in a day depends upon the number of your crew and their agility.

It is usual to average around fifteen to twenty locks a day once you get used to the physical exertion involved. Moving a boat through locks is not a particularly strenuous occupation but after your first few days you realize what sort of physical condition you are in. It is wise to take it easy at first.

Speed limits are as follows:	
Canals	$3\frac{1}{4}$ knots
Seine 20 tons and over	$13\frac{1}{2}$ knots
when passing	8 knots

10 tons and over	8	knots upstream
	$9\frac{3}{4}$	knots downstream
In Paris	$6\frac{1}{2}$	knots
Rhône	$13\frac{1}{2}$	knots
when passing	8	knots
Marne	$6\frac{1}{2}$	knots
General Limit	6	knots

The canal speed limit of just over 3 knots does not seem to be very closely observed by commercial traffic. In some of the narrower canals a speed of 5 knots can set up a considerable wash, and where damage to the banks is likely to result you should slow down; wherever the wash of your craft is likely to inconvenience others you should also slow down, in fact you should use your judgement and show consideration at all times. It will be seen that speed limits in the rivers are higher than in the canals but, whenever you are in doubt, you can use the barges as your guide in this matter.

In planning your cruise it will pay to consult as many maps and guide books as possible so that you go through, and near, most places of interest. The Michelin sectional maps are so useful for this purpose that the appropriate sectional map numbers have been placed against each place name shown in the **Route Details Section.** If you write to the local *Syndicats d'Initiative* of the towns along your planned route they will be pleased to send you information regarding items of interest in their area and of events taking place at the time of your proposed visit. Minutes spent in advance planning will repay with hours of interest and pleasure on the cruise. Somehow this planning seems to be more worthwhile with a cruise than with a motor tour, maybe because you cruise along the waterways in such a leisurely fashion that stopping is no inconvenience, and you get used to stopping for locks anyhow.

Cruising the French canals is the most delightful experience, catering for every taste; an active holiday for the active and a leisurely one for the leisurely, all rolled into one.

To get the most out of your exploring you need a bicycle for each person on board; a place on deck can usually be found for them. The Michelin maps show all the byways, and to coast along the country lanes to do your shopping at out of the way villages is a delight. There will be no shortage of volunteers to pedal along some grassy towpath in the clear morning air to fetch the bread and milk. Shopping bags are no weight on the handlebars. When water and fuel have to be carried any distance the bike will be worth its weight in Puligny-Montrachet. And if you wish to make quicker progress through some relatively uninteresting section, a crew member can easily cycle ahead along the towpath to prepare the locks for your coming.

Having planned your route you will obviously want to stick to it when you arrive in France or your planning will be very largely wasted.

The details given against the place names in the **Route Details Section** are not by any means comprehensive, but it is hoped that the brief data given will arouse your interest sufficiently for you to want to seek further information. I am indebted to my numerous friends in many Syndicats d'Initiative for supplying the details shown. At each of the places named, whether described or not, it is understood that at least a shop will be nearby, and usually there will be much more.

No special skill is needed to handle a boat on the French canals. Any active couple with the intelligence to navigate a car will find no difficulty in handling a motor cruiser. If you doubt this, consider the tens of thousands who drive a motor cruiser for the first time on the Norfolk Broads or on the Thames—or in the French canals (see 'Cruising Holidays'). There is a pointer in one French canal cruise holiday brochure that states: 'previous cruising experience (though not essential) is an asset'.

I do not suggest that anyone without experience, setting out on

1. Cycle along the grassy towpath for bread and milk in the morning.

a cruise of the French canals, should cross the Channel unaccompanied from England, although many do. I do not have to think very hard to recall three, six, a dozen modest adventurers we have met in France and the Mediterranean in their first sailing boat, having had no experience whatever before setting out.

Whether or not it is wise to do this is another matter; perhaps the man who stops too long to wonder if he might learn to manage a boat does not have it in him to be even a modest adventurer. I would repeat again and again that the biggest factor in the whole business of going off on a worthwhile cruise is the making of the decision to do it.

Perhaps the hesitant by nature always stand too much in awe of experience. Put out of your mind that great intelligence or ability is needed to navigate or to handle a boat. Professional skippers are no Einsteins, and as for the amateurs, an hour in a marina watching the mooring antics would convince you that many existing yachtsmen deserve to be carrying L-plates.

Make up your mind that you can master boat handling and you will; if you have an experienced friend to help you, so much the better. The important thing to acquire in your own home cruising area is the ability to handle your boat precisely. Common sense conquers most problems once you can handle your boat with certainty.

The *Certificat de Capacité* (proof of competence) is no longer required of the skippers of small boats entering France. If it is ever called for it will be in a place where navigation is difficult or dangerous, and in such places it should always be possible to find a pilot.

What sort of person goes cruising on the inland waterways of France? One of the many pleasant features of cruising life is that you make friends immediately when you stop by another boat; but if it was possible to analyze all the gossiping that we have done in this way over the years, I do not think that any particular age group, type or class of person would emerge.

If the cruising life attracts all ages and types, there is one thing, at least, that most have in common, and that is the ability to get on with one another. If this quality is not very apparent at the beginning of a cruise it will certainly blossom during it. A boat is a wonderful place for developing a deeper understanding of one another; in the confinement of a cabin you simply have to get on together, and most people do.

4 Suitable and Unsuitable Boats

What boat to choose? Sail or power? New or second-hand?
If you are a beginner you will obviously have less to learn if you
buy a motor cruiser rather than a sailing yacht; but this consideration cannot be of the greatest importance because beginners are
sailing away in sailing yachts every day of the week.

Quite apart from the relative merits of sailing versus motor
cruising, a motor cruiser will have roomier accommodation for a
given overall length than a sailing boat. The sailing boat hull needs
to be a 'sailing shape' whereas the motor cruising hull does not
need such fine underwater lines. The comparatively restricted
accommodation of a sailing yacht is further restricted by stowage
room needed for sails and gear. The cockpit space needed for
managing the business of sailing can be used for accommodation in
a motor cruiser.

You would only buy a sailing boat if you were keen to enjoy
sailing at times when you were not inland cruising. At these times
the handling of a sailing boat involves your family, for one member
usually attends to sail changing while another minds the helm.
In a motor cruiser, only the one person at the wheel is involved.

These are all general considerations to be borne in mind and do
not refer specifically to selecting the most suitable craft in which to
explore the French canals; for this purpose alone there is no doubt
that a motor cruiser would be the obvious choice.

If, however, you feel that you would like to sail sometimes and
explore the inland waterways on other occasions, then there is no
difficulty in unstepping the mast of a suitable compromise sailing
yacht when you want to use it for canal cruising. Big sailing yachts
with tall masts would obviously not be suitable for the inland
waterways because of their deep draft. In addition to this, no sailing
yacht whose mast height greatly exceeds the LOA of the boat

should be selected as a compromise canal cruiser; apart from being a nuisance when manoeuvring, the overhang can easily cause damage, not only to the overhanging section, but to the whole mast and to everything to which it is attached.

Most entry ports into France have yacht clubs where masts can not only be unstepped, but stored. In Le Havre, for instance, this can be arranged at the Petit Port by the Capitain du Port on the quay from whom you book a time for going under the crane. The last time (June 1981) I was there in a ketch the charge was 150 FF for the two masts and the staff were most kind and helpful.

In ports where a crane is not available it is quite often possible to go alongside a British merchant ship to have the lift made by the ship's derrick. If neither crane nor derrick is available there will always be some convenient height nearby from which to exert the necessary leverage and control. A bridge over the waterway is ideal. Spare blocks and suitable rope should be carried for rigging up a pulley arrangement (tackle) to the bridge; the right-size trestles for stowing the mast on deck should be made up before leaving home.

Before considering specific craft it should be mentioned that catamarans are not suitable for cruising the French canals by reason of their beam; averaging nearly half of the LOA, this beam would prevent entry into the small space often left for pleasure craft in the busier commercial locks. On the narrower waterways, passing other craft would present problems. Many catamarans have made passages through the French canals, but I would not recommend them as a suitable choice.

Trimarans, with a beam often equal to almost two-thirds of their LOA, would not even get into the majority of the locks.

The ideal craft is a twin-screw motor cruiser with inside and outside steering positions and controls, but only if it is a craft with propellers protected, either by the sort of metal guards that you see on barges or by the actual position of the propellers in the shape of the hull. If a propeller is so sited that it is the first thing to touch the sloping side of a lock, the boat is going to need plenty of spare propellers.

The same objections, indeed more so, apply to outdrives, inboard/outboards, transom, stern drives, or whatever other name is given to outside drive units, to my mind unsuitable for the French canals. I have seen them caught on the sills of descending locks and am convinced that the less you have 'outside' of your boat the less likely you are to run into trouble. Even if remote controls could bring outside drive units completely inboard, instead of raising them, the point is that there is rarely any advance warning of the time when this might be necessary.

Protection is, therefore, essential for any yacht with exposed propellers. If you have a choice between single or twin, single is perfectly adequate for the French canals, and obviously more economical. A twin screw is more manoeuvrable, although a good man will manage a single screw better than a poorer man with a twin.

Many people write to ask me what is the most suitable craft for them and I am happy to oblige. I need to know how many there will be in the crew, how much money it is proposed to spend, and the extent of sailing or cruising experience.

It is hardly necessary for me to stress, I hope, that you should never buy a second-hand boat without a professional survey.

Before you consider buying any yacht or motor cruiser it is a good idea to study a 'catalogue' of new craft available. With suitable diffidence I may, perhaps, mention that these are set out in detail in *Bristow's Book of Yachts* brought up to date in each annual edition and available from booksellers or, in case of difficulty, from Moorhouse, Lower Kingston, Ringwood, Hants price £7.95 plus postage.

For anyone seeking a second-hand class yacht and keen to find out what they cost new, there are back numbers of *Bristow's Book* available for the years 1967, 1968, 1969, 1970, 1975, 1977, 1978/79, 1979/80 at £5 each from the above address.

The question of British Registry of British owned craft in France was the subject of much argument and discussion in 1980; indeed non-registered British craft in the South of France were actually seized by over-zealous French Customs officers. A compromise has now been reached granting dispensation until 1 January 1984, after which date all British owned craft in France must be British registered. Meanwhile it is said that a simpler form of registry is being worked out in time for the proposed date of enforcement.

The R.Y.A. has been active in protecting the rights of yachtsmen in this matter of registration and if you are not a member may I suggest that you join and thus help the cause. The address is Royal Yachting Association, Victoria Way, Woking, Surrey GU21 1EQ and they are always most helpful and willing to advise you on the current situation regarding documentation needed for craft entering France (and, of course, on many other matters). Indeed, as you probably know, the R.Y.A. has been the provider of acceptable 'papers' for unregistered craft entering France for many years.

In considering a suitable boat for the waterways you will be thinking in terms of living onboard for several months at a time and you will want as much room as you can afford, and certainly headroom; an aft cabin is a good idea for families with children or for two families. It also makes for easier living to have the separate bedroom that an aft cabin makes possible.

Aft cabins entail centre cockpits, of course, and you have the choice of open cockpit, wheelshelter or enclosed wheelhouse. If sailing you cannot expect to engage in much agile sail changing with an enclosed wheelhouse but when sailing this type of craft the sails are usually sheeted home and left while the craft motor-sails on a passage making course. Some centre open cockpit sailing craft of about 36ft LOA and above have an under cockpit passageway from the saloon to the aft cabin. Although this is an ideal arrangement once onboard, the provision of this passageway necessitates such a high freeboard that getting on and off the boat needs some agility. You should bear in mind this question of freeboard when you are going about the delightful business of choosing your dream yacht for the French waterways. The seller of any 'high-out-of-the-water' dream yacht will have thoughtfully provided a stepped platform alongside for your ease of access and descent when you come to view; but when emergencies arise later and you need to quickly leap off or on there will be no gentleman alongside with a stepped platform. You will need to be stepping off and on at high speed on occasions and you will be glad to have chosen a boat that allows you, not to mention your lady crew, to do this easily.

Enclosed wheelhouse motor cruisers and motor sailers have, as the name implies, all enclosed accommodation so that you can go from the aft sleeping cabin, preferably with its own toilet and shower compartment, up to the wheelhouse saloon with dining table and seating from which you can watch the world go by; down to the galley and then to the forward sleeping cabin, also with its own toilet and shower compartment. The wheelhouse will have sliding doors on each side giving easy accessibility to port and starboard side decks. You should really look for a yacht with a secondary, outside, steering position as well.

Cockpit canopies and steering shelters are available in all shapes and sizes to provide part or complete protection. It seems that as yachtsmen get older so do they like to be protected by a bit of woodwork and I must say that there is a lot to be said for an enclosed wheelhouse when you are living onboard for a long time. (When I am in aft cabin open cockpit craft it always seems to be pouring with rain whenever I want to go from the aft bedroom to the forward accommodation—dressed in my pyjamas needless to say.)

Two toilets make for harmony, two toilets **and** showers make for luxury indeed, but naturally you have to watch the water supply, pumps, heaters, drain away.

Shallow draft or bilge keel craft are an advantage in the waterways because they enable you to go alongside attractive river banks and villages denied to a deeper draft. For the ideal French waterway yacht I think that a 4ft draft is about right despite the average waterway depth of two metres. I have taken yachts drawing 5ft 6in plus through the waterways without trouble but with such a draft one's stopping places are limited. Retractable keels are not often seen but they are eminently suitable. A diesel engine is preferred because they seem to be less troublesome and go on 'plonk-plonk-plonking' away for ever, it seems, at quite a considerable saving on petrol, (in France at the time of writing—August 1981—at least).

Glass fibre, wood or steel or ferro for the hull? The choice is up to you. No one material is better than any other for the waterways; fenders or tyres should take what bashing is encountered. Most people prefer not to have a grp interior but most grp craft now boast that their interiors are made of a strange new material known as wood.

For many yachtsmen the most preferred material would be a wooden hull but building costs are all against the return of the shipwright, the cost of a wooden craft being half as much again as steel and often of grp. When you consider that there are shipwrights and joiners out of work, or engaged in non-yacht building jobs, it is sad indeed; men with the skills in their hands to fashion beautiful craft should not be on the scrapheap, nor failing to pass on their skills to a succeeding—and as it happens, idle—generation.

When we first started exploring the European Waterways, (about a hundred years ago it seems) everybody doing it seemed to be poor like us and people were in boats that had cost less than a thousand pounds. Nowadays the boats sought are of utmost luxury compared with those far off days; separate cabins with headroom throughout, kitchens better equipped than many ashore, showers, several toilets. If you are going to live onboard for a long time you want to take along as many comforts as possible and most people do.

Many more people approaching retirement are now seeking to spend their early retired years in cruising the European waterways and wintering in the Mediterranean. I have been retained to find suitable boats for many. 'For a year or so, maybe', they protest tentatively, but years later I receive cards from happy, bronzed nautical tramps who could never consider giving up the marine gipsy life and whose only regret is that they did not embark upon it years earlier.

An odd observation, but one that my wife and I have made frequently, is that personal relationships improve when confined to the waterway life. You would imagine the reverse to be the case, indeed we have all heard women protesting that 'they do not know what they will do when they are shut up with him all day long on his retirement'—and they are usually referring to life in a house! The intimacy of the boating life must act like an emotional pressure cooker bringing out only the best; we have seen the most unlikely couples wandering ashore hand in hand . . .

When you plan on boating in retirement and want to carry your wife along with you, you must plan for comfort first of all; you can forget all about sailing on your ear. Give your wife a superb kitchen and dining area, a comfortable bedroom, toilet and shower and then—and only then—can you start deciding how much sailing performance and paraphernalia you can wrap around that.

Even for wives who openly object to sailing, who have simply never gone along with a man's boating ideas at all, there is still the avenue of persuasion represented by the inland waterways of Europe . . . Obviously you would not take her across Seine Bay by way of introduction; but to have the boat alongside some charming French village where you have arranged for the official embarkation, dinner ashore perhaps, and then next day to commence gliding through the beauty of France, bounce-free and passing by a never ending panorama of interest . . . you can more easily than you think have your wife hooked on the boating life. By the time you get to the Mediterranean the boat will have become a way of life for her, the odd bounce will be accepted.

By the time you get to the Mediterranean you will both also be very much fitter and perhaps this is the time to mention that if you have been accustomed to a sedentary life you should retire to the boating life by easy stages. If you make yourself competent at handling your craft, the passage through the many locks should present no physical stresses but after the first few days of rope throwing and hauling and maybe some lock ladder climbing you can expect to be exhausted. Then after a day of rest and recovery and a bottle or so of Côtes du Rhône you recover; but you will not fully enjoy the French canals if you try to do too much too soon. Your

choice of boat is all important from what one might call the
conservation of energy point of view; and the less agile you are the
more you must consider this aspect when choosing your boat. When
I am asked to find a suitable craft, as I frequently am since this is my
other activity, one of the first considerations I take into account is the
physical capability of the buyer and his crew in relation to the boat
to be chosen. I make no apology for emphasizing that if you choose a
boat that is 'too much for you' your European waterway adventures
will be more stress and strain than pleasure; if you choose a boat that
is totally within your physical control and capability your European
waterway cruises will fulfil your pleasantest dreams.

Over the years we have met a number of people in a variety of
boats, and it may be of interest to recall what sort of craft others
have picked as their choice for the inland waterways.

On their way down the Rhine, and so to Utrecht in Holland, we
met a charming couple; they were not old although they were both
over seventy. They were in a single-screw, 28ft diesel cruiser with
a centre cockpit, open except for a steering shelter, but a fitting
cover made it virtually enclosed when necessary. The forepeak was
used for stowage; the saloon was fitted with a dinette, galley,
enclosed toilet, and shelves and lockers. The separate aft cabin was
used for sleeping only. There were no side decks, stanchions, or
guard rails, just a bare foothold on which to scramble forward and
aft to handle mooring lines. They had been cruising for five months,
all inland, and were returning home. Each year for the last ten
years they had taken a six months' cruise in the same boat. In the
neat cabin we were shown photographs of their fourteen grand-
children. This youthful grandmother announced that she was going
back home to learn French and also how to swim so that she could
get even more enjoyment out of her future cruises.

A 43ft diesel ketch was the choice of a fifty-year-old printer we
met in the Bourgogne; at first sight she seemed to be too high out of
the water and the owner confirmed that he had had a little trouble
in squeezing under some of the bridges, on one occasion carrying
rocks on board until the ketch was low enough in the water. We
suggested that it might have been less trouble if he had thought to
invite a few heavy locals on board for a drink. With his wife and
teenage son he was on his way to the Greek Islands, having sold his
business. The ketch had three separate sleeping cabins and a
bathroom, a luxurious counter-top galley, roomy wheelhouse with
a monstrous single diesel under; wide side decks with a firm rail all
round. It had cost £10000. The printer had never sailed a boat

before in his life, but his son had some experience of crewing.

It is not unusual to meet owners without previous experience. We always seem to meet a few Americans in Paris who have just bought their first boat in England and made their first ever sail across the Channel; in England, apparently, there is a better selection of second-hand boats at better prices than anywhere else in the world.

One such American was kind enough to offer me advice on cruising in general and marine engines in particular; in fact he went to the trouble of overhauling my engine for me, but I was able to get it going again properly a month or so later. Around thirty years of age he was with his wife and baby daughter, plus a Cairn terrier called Harold Wilson. The boat he had chosen was a second-hand Fairey Atalanta sloop with a Perkins 4.107 engine. The separate after cabin was useful for the child, the rest of the accommodation roomy, if a little like the inside of a submarine. These are the craft already mentioned, with retractable bilge keels which can be wound up into the hull leaving a draft of only 38cm. This particular boat had cost something under £2000 and was quite a good buy for the purpose. The owner explained that they had had a rough ride across the Channel, entering France at Dunkirk.

An 18ft sloop, built thirty years ago, was the choice of another American we met. Her centre keel drew over 91cm and she was a neat little boat of character; but there was barely sitting headroom below, even just inside the cabin. To get to the toilet forward involved getting ready in a jack-knife position and forcing one's self backwards like driving in a wedge. She had cost the proud owner something under £1000.

An elderly American and his wife had chosen as their first boat a bare hull fitted with a diesel engine. Their idea was to make it habitable as they went along. Ketch rigged, it had good, wide decks. There was a great deal of space below; the galley was temporary until the proper accommodation was built. The bunk was temporary. Everything was temporary except the toilet standing up like a lonely throne. Only the handiest of handymen should consider buying bare hulls, and they should not consider moving an inch from their home base until they are fully completed. This American had never sailed a boat before in his life, and explained that he had had a bad time crossing the Channel, entering France at Dunkirk.

Practically all the Americans we met had selected sailboats, with the vague idea of going down through France, down to Gibraltar, round to the Canaries, and across the Atlantic. Few of them had any previous experience.

Most British yachtsmen going through the French canals for the first time do so in sailing yachts; most British yachtsmen in the French canals for the second (and subsequent) time are in motor cruisers. Most Dutch, Danish, Norwegian, and Swedish yachtsmen in the French canals are in motor cruisers. These observations are only based on our own experience and conversations with others and must obviously be discounted to that extent.

A single-hander that we particularly liked was a seventy-three-year-old Englishman in a 48ft steel cruiser; equipped with twin BMC Captain diesels, he had been cruising in the waterways for five months and twenty-eight days, and his 'time' was up. With all enclosed accommodation, centre wheelhouse, large after cabin as a permanent bedroom, and a big living space forward, it was, of course, luxury for one. The owner was going to hand in the ship's papers to the French Customs and leave his boat in France until he could return again. He had no fear of the Channel crossing, for he had fitted himself up with an auto-pilot and, as he said, 'just walked up and down with a telescope under his arm'. But with many years' experience of cruising the French canals, he still preferred to leave his boat in France.

To mention a dozen (or more) Scandinavian owners that we have met would not entail mentioning a dozen (or more) different types of craft. They all seem to go in for the (more or less) standard diesel cruisers, some of which are familiar to us, such as the Sagaling already described. All fairly similar in layout, with forepeak, saloon, open cockpit, or wheel shelter, and some with an aft cabin, some without. Variations on single or twin engines, inboard or outdrive are available, but the majority of Scandinavian boats that we met were fitted with single inboard engines and all were diesel. How much, and what quality of this type of boat you get, depends upon how much you pay. The open shelter type of cockpit seems to be the most popular; the heavy canvas cover that zips around it is most effective.

A forty-year-old ex-businessman from Arhus invited us on board his 32ft glass-fibre diesel cruiser for a drink one evening. It was pouring with rain, and as we stepped under the canvas cover and into the dark cockpit we could see down into the after cabin where two boys were lying cosily in their bunks, reading by the light of a centre table-light. Down from the wheelhouse, forward into the main cabin, we were offered the two seats on one side of the dinette and our host and his wife sat on the other side. Along one side of the boat opposite to the dinette was the galley, and when we praised the layout they told us that they had bought the boat from Klaus Baess, a name well known at the London Boat Show.

Over brandy (has there ever been a teetotal yachtsman?) and coffee we learned that they had sold up their business and house in Denmark, bought this boat and sailed away for two years, this apparently being the minimum time under Danish law to qualify for certain tax concessions. They showed us colour pictures of their former home, a small mansion with green lawns and beautiful gardens, and we marvelled that our hostess had been able to give up so much for life on a small boat with two young children. At that moment there was a small cry from the forepeak ahead and our hostess got up; they had a small baby as well!

It had been difficult at first she conceded. But now they all loved the freedom of the boating life so much that they did not want to go back to any house. They had spent the winter in Spain, far enough down to ensure permanent sunshine. Photographs of their Christmas dinner party showed them in the cockpit in swimsuits.

Of all the different people we have met in all the different types of boats, none have admitted to any regrets. All agreed that the biggest factor in the whole enterprise was the making of the decision to do it.

Getting away from it all is a thought that occurs to most of us from time to time. But the opportunity to do so is not something that just comes along, it has to be made. And because no chance can be seen of getting away for good, this is no excuse for not getting away for as long a period as you can manage.

5 Now you can get back up the Rhône

I do not believe that such a vast achievement as the taming of the Rhône should be taken for granted, however, and I feel that every user of this waterway should be aware of the vision, enterprise, courage and effort of the Frenchmen who created it. I am indebted to the *Compagnie Nationale du Rhône* who have kindly supplied me with the information contained in this chapter.

In previous editions I referred to the Rhône as a 'slippery slope'; the inference being that once one left Lyon and passed through the Pierre-Bénite Lock to embark on the downstream passage of the Rhône, for most craft it was a one-way journey, as most craft would not possess the power to get up again. Going down has never been a problem; unless you count as problems raging torrents, midstream rocks, wildly varying depths of water, shifting sand-banks, mud-banks and gravel-banks.

Although smallest of the three principal river basins of France, the Rhône in former days presented many difficulties to navigation. Apart from the speed and irregularity of the Rhône current, shipping was further hazarded by the formation of gravel-banks, aided by the Alpine 'feeders' Isère and Durance bringing down large amounts of mud, gravel and flood water from melted snow; the Cévennes streams, Ardèche and Gard, on the right bank also caused sudden rises and falls.

The giant power of the river has always been utilised to sweep man and cargoes down from Lyon to the sea. This giant power has its origins in the greenish ice of the Rhône Glacier, barely fifty miles from the origin of the north-flowing Rhine; by the Belvedere Inn on the Funka Pass in the Swiss Alps a stream comes rushing out that is the beginning of the mighty Rhône. Spring sunshine melts the Alpine snows and through meadows dotted with blue gentian, yellow mountain saxifrage and dark red dwarf primula the river gathers strength and is joined by other streams from the mountains on both sides.

Twenty-eight miles from its source, at the town of Brig, the Rhône has already dropped 4,000 feet. By the time it reaches Lake Geneva it has travelled 105 miles, all too swift and too steep for navigation. Forty-five miles across, at the other end of the lake, locks take over control. Twelve miles from Geneva the Rhône becomes French and they immediately put it to work; a few miles inside the French border is the huge Genissiat Dam.

Coming up has always been the ordeal and upstream traffic has been negligible. Until the advent of steam it took thirty or forty horses to tow one barge up to Lyon. The difficulties were so considerable that many cargoes were despatched downstream on collapsible rafts that were dismantled at the Mediterranean end. Then steam power took over from the horse and from the collapsible raft. Rhône navigation became of great importance during the first half of the 19th century. Then the Marseille-Lyon railway opened and Rhône navigation suffered a virtual collapse.

At the end of the century the industrial potential of hydro-electricity was realized; the energy producing possibilities of the Rhône . . . coupled with the transformation of the agriculture of the valley by the development of an irrigation system . . . coupled with the development of the river into an international waterway . . . these considerations resulted in the 'Rhône formula' by which the river would be developed by means of the profits received from hydro-electricity.

A law was passed in 1921 granting development powers to various interests. Discussions and negotiations ensued. In 1933 the *Compagnie Nationale du Rhône* was created with the stature of a limited company, a 'Company of General Interest'. In 1934 the CNR received the general concession for the development of the Rhône; it was a company with the characteristics of a limited company, with a capital of 24 million francs divided into 2,400,000 shares! A company in which the following local interests participated:

the Department of the Seine, a large consumer of energy
the Department, Communes, Chambers of Commerce and
    Chambers of Agriculture of the Rhône Valley
the Paris-Lyon-Mediterranée Railway Company (forseeing the
    electrification of the Paris–Marseille line)
and companies involved in transport and electricity.

In 1937 the railways were nationalized and the P.L.M. became the S.N.C.F. In 1946 electricity was nationalized and *Electricité de France* became the interested party in that sphere.

C.N.R. conforms in certain aspects to a nationalized company. The government guarantees borrowing since the profits made from the sale of the Rhône energy must be used to benefit navigation and agriculture. The C.N.R. may not charge tolls for navigating the Rhône nor for agricultural use of the water.

C.N.R.'s general programme included the construction of twenty-one combined developments (grouping primarily barrages, dammed reservoirs, diversion canals, navigation locks, works assuring drainage) which principally feed nineteen major hydro-electric stations, seven of which are situated on the Upper Rhône above Lyon, the other twelve being on the Lower Rhône.

The impressive figures of electric energy production envisaged are outside the scope of these comments. From the navigation point of view the first priority was to be given to the construction of a waterway with a complete canal system stretching 310km in length from Lyon to the Mediterranean (Port St. Louis du Rhône). This waterway with a complete canal system stretching 310km in length locks.

The creation of surrounding port zones and industrial zones was envisaged, increased possibilities for irrigation and the consquent improvement of agriculture, protection against flooding, stabilisation of the water table and the creation of nautical facilities.

From the outset the C.N.R.'s interest in Rhône navigation was demonstrated with the construction of Port Edouard Herriot, in a suburb south of Lyon, directly below the junction of the Rhône and Saône rivers; begun in 1934 the port was put into full operation in 1973 (having been considerably enlarged in 1966).

Construction of the GENISSIAT (1937–1948) and SEYSSEL (1951) barrages do not concern us here since they are situated in the gorges of the Upper Rhône and were created purely for hydro-electric potential.

Development of the central portion of the Lower Rhône, between Isère and Ardèche, took place between 1947 and 1968.

In 1947 construction began at Donzère-Mondragon, after which developments at Montélimar, Baix-Le Logis Neuf, Beauchastel and Bourg-lès-Valence proceeded. To illustrate the scale of this gigantic project it may be of interest to mention the detail involved in one construction. Five years of effort (1947–1952) at DONZÈRE-MONDRAGON created the following major projects:

The reservoir-barrage, raising the water level by 5m at low water and producing a dammed reservoir of approximately 10km.

The diversion canal, short circuiting 31km of the river, including a 17km lead-in canal and an 11km escape canal. The intake of water feeding the lead-in canal includes two branches; a navigable branch,

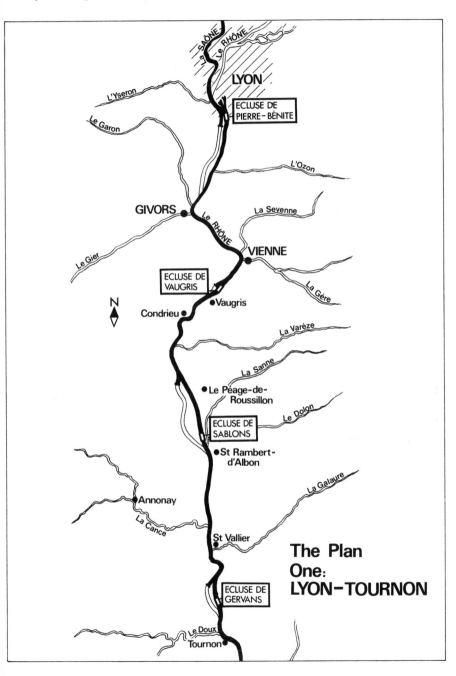

The Plan
One:
LYON–TOURNON

wide and not very deep, allowing for the passage of one-third of the flow; the other branch handling the other two-thirds. The lock allows for a difference in level of 26m (85ft!). The ability to rapidly fill and empty the lock chambers of a capacity of almost 60,000m³ without noticeable effect on the water level was solved in ingenious fashion.

The building of Donzère-Mondragon took a work force of 6,800 which, with their families, meant that over 10,000 people had to be accommodated in new sites built nearby.

The MONTELIMAR development (1953–1957) included an intake of Rhône water at right angles to Rochemaure and a diversion canal close to 14km in length on the left bank of the Rhône. The lock allows for a difference in level of 19m (62ft).

BAIX-LE-LOGIS NEUF was opened in 1960.

BEAUCHASTEL in 1963, (the only development whose diversion is on the right bank of the Rhône) and BOURG-LES-VALENCE in 1968, each with an average drop of 11/12m (36ft–39ft).

Thus the works of the central third of the Rhône were completed.

At Baix-le-Logis Neuf the junction of the Drôme was made to take place in the reservoir. At Bourg-lès-Valence the Isère was absorbed in the canal; the central portion of the lead-in canal being, in fact, the lower riverbed of the Isère.

Whilst the central part was thus being developed an even more ambitious project was taking place on the Rhône immediately downstream with its junction with the Saône. This development at PIERRE-BENITE (1962–1966), established a continuous canal reach of 21km on the Rhône and the Saône up to the lock at Couzon and did away with two old locks on the Saône at La Mulatière and Ile-Barbe. In this way Pierre-Bénite became the unifying link for the Port of Lyon and the rivers Rhône and Saône. (The works at Pierre-Bénite also provided excavated material on which was built the huge Rhône-Alps Refinery at Feyzin and transformed a deserted and marshy region, ravaged by Rhône floods into an industrial zone.)

Completion of the Rhône developments below Lyon were considered with regard for industrial advancement, for creating a steel industry at Fos, for increasing the transport capacity of the Rhône from 15 million tons per year to over 50 million tons per year with the doubling of locks.

VALLABREGUES (1966–1970) extended the drop from Avignon to Tarascon-Beaucaire in a flat plain of negligible decline. This

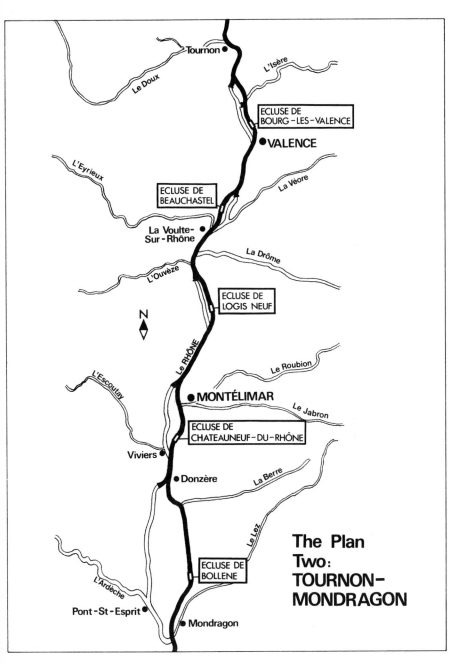

Tournon

L'Isère

Le Doux

ECLUSE DE
BOURG – LES – VALENCE

●VALENCE

L'Eyrieux

La Véore

ECLUSE DE
BEAUCHASTEL

La Voulte-
Sur-Rhône ●

La Drôme

L'Ouvèze

ECLUSE DE
LOGIS NEUF

N

Le RHÔNE

Le Roubion

L'Escoutay

●MONTÉLIMAR

Le Jabron

ECLUSE DE
CHATEAUNEUF–DU–RHÔNE

Viviers ●

● Donzère

La Berre

Le Lez

The Plan
Two:
TOURNON-
MONDRAGON

ECLUSE DE
BOLLENE

L'Ardèche

Pont-St-Esprit ●

● Mondragon

development canalized the river for 34km. Although the earthworks moved and materials used at Vallabrègues were comparable to those at Donzère-Mondragon the workforce never exceeded 1,800 as opposed to the 6,800 employed at Donzère-Mondragon; increased productivity resulted in 33 months being spent at Vallabrègues compared to 50 months at Donzère-Mondragon. Hence within the space of 15 years the manpower needed for construction could be reduced in the ratio of 6:1.

SAINT VALLIER (1969–1973) is characterized by its long reservoirs between Saint-Rambert d'Albon and Serves and short diversion. The drop varies between 10m (33ft) and 11,5m (38ft). This operation lengthened the continuous canalization of the Rhône to 134km from the 115km at Mondragon.

At Le Palier d'Arles (1971–1973) it was a question of developing the Rhône riverbed by dredging, between the restoration of water at Vallabrègues and the Petit Rhône up to the region at St. Gilles. (From then it was no longer possible to lock through from the Rhône into the Beaucaire Sète Canal at Beaucaire.) Joining of the Rhône canal at Sète by means of the new lock saw the beginning of the international use of this waterway.

The AVIGNON (1971–1973) development included a dammed reservoir over 10km in length.

The opening of CADEROUSSE removed the last remaining obstacle to navigation on the downstream third of the Rhône. The joining achieved by this lock between the developed sections of the downstream third and central third created an uninterrupted distance of 249km between the Mediterranean and St. Rambert d'Albon.

LE PEAGE-DE-ROUSILION (1973–1974) includes a dammed reservoir extending for 25km and a diversion canal 11km in length.

VAUGRIS (at K.33) involved the section of the river between Pierre-Bénite and Condrieu; this was the last link in the chain between the Mediterranean and Lyon, a total distance of 310km. Although it was only a short section that remained uncompleted, and the temporary channel round was quite straightforward, it seemed to remain uncompleted for a long time, arousing anxieties in the minds of Rhône cruising yachtsmen out of proportion to the 20km involved. But now it is done.

Work on the development of Port Zones proceeds at Portes-lès-Valence, Montélimar, Avignon, Beaucaire, Arles. Fulfilment of the North-Sea-Mediterranean waterway dream continues.

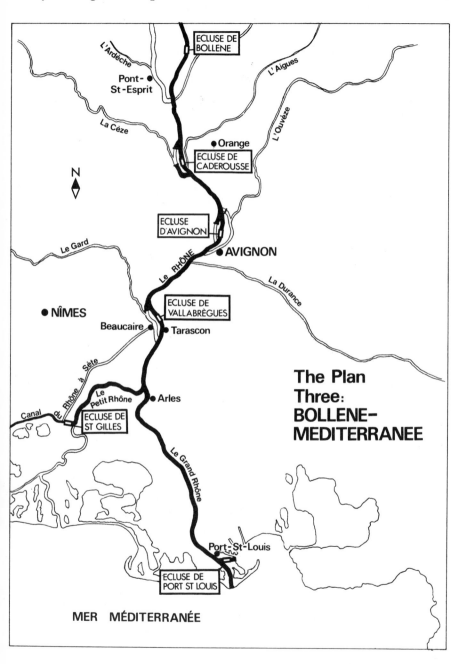

ECLUSE DE
BOLLENE

L'Ardèche

Pont-
St-Esprit

L'Aigues

La Cèze

L'Ouvèze

● Orange

ECLUSE DE
CADEROUSSE

N

ECLUSE
D'AVIGNON

Le RHÔNE

Le Gard

● AVIGNON

Le RHÔNE

La Durance

● NÎMES

ECLUSE DE
VALLABRÈGUES

Beaucaire ● ● Tarascon

Canal

du Rhône à Sète

Le
Petit Rhône

● Arles

ECLUSE DE
ST GILLES

**The Plan
Three:
BOLLENE-
MEDITERRANEE**

Le Grand Rhône

Port-St-Louis

ECLUSE DE
PORT ST LOUIS

MER   MÉDITERRANÉE

And now you can get back up the Rhône . . . IF you can make 7 knots that is. At times your speed over the ground will appear to be negligible but for almost the whole distance the flow will be smooth and controlled and calm looking. The surging, soaring passage of yesterday is forgotten.

But the current still runs strongly and before you undertake a passage of the Rhône, either up or down, you should ensure that the engine of your craft is in good order; a broken fan belt, dirty fuel or blocked filter in the cooling system can be unfortunate at any time but would easily spell disaster on the Rhône.

However confident you are in the efficiency of your engine(s) you must have anchor and chain ready; if you had to use it it might not hold but at least it would swing you round and check you. Steering as though going ahead at least you would have a chance of avoiding the piers of bridges, etc.

It is a good idea to make the passage of the Rhône in company with another yacht so that in the event of engine failure one can help by 'supplying brakes' to the other.

It is not necessary now to employ a pilot. But take care, particularly in the short, uncanalized section.

You must also be sure that you have adequate fuel, taking spare cans onboard if necessary. The withdrawal of F.O.D. (*fuel oil doméstique*) for use in pleasure craft is mentioned elsewhere, but the difficulties of obtaining fuel are noticeable between Chalon-sur-Saône and Port St. Louis. The same remarks apply to petrol.

On the Bollène-Mediterranean section of the Rhône map, (as on other maps), you will see that the river is shown as flowing straight down to the Mediterranean as indeed it does or, at least, it finally spreads its way there. But, in fact, the final section of the Rhône is not a waterway to anywhere for traffic intending to 'turn right' has already done so at the Petit Rhône, (or previously Beaucaire-Sète), and traffic intending to 'turn left' has already done so at Arles-Fos or at Port St. Louis. Even in this area the river is already between half a mile and a mile wide in places; down the final 6km, below Port St. Louis, the mighty Rhône finally dissipates itself fanwise in separate and changing and uncharted streams; all we found was a nowhere of desolation, even by Camargue standards, shifting sands and silt pushing ever seawards.

6 Equipment

Some equipment that you will need to take your boat safely to France will not be needed for your inland cruise, for instance:

Compass	Parallel ruler
Hand-bearing compass	Dividers, etc.
Log	Life-jackets
RDF	Charts, sailing directions
Radar reflector	Kit of flares

On cruising into the beautiful waterways of France you can forget all about plotting courses, and fixes, and sail changing, bouncing around and hanging on. You can forget all about the need to work out your direction—it is there, ahead, the water-road referred to by Georges Normand in his introduction.

The equipment needed will be confined to the business of protecting your yacht against the odd encounter with other craft and with lock walls, of providing adequate securing and getting ashore facilities, of fuel and water transport, and of safety onboard.

Adequate fenders are necessary, a minimum of four, large, sausage shape, and must be carried for the times when you go alongside yachts with gleaming topsides or into yacht harbours. But for the canals generally and commercial harbours, there is so much oil and grime about that white fenders would be ruined very quickly. Motor tyres are the obvious answer, and since any garage will be delighted to get rid of any number of old ones for nothing, there is no point in stinting on them. If you reckon on one for each 1,25m of waterline each side, this should be sufficient. You will need to 'string them up' quite substantially, for they sometimes come under considerable strain when being squeezed along the sides of steel barges. And they can be easily broken off on entering UP-locks where a crew member is being put ashore with a warp; for the lock ladder is usually just inside beyond the lock gate and in manoeuvring to put your crew on the ladder you must obviously be close in, so close that tyres get pressed into the gate recess and held there while the yacht moves on. It does not often happen, indeed after only a little practice the tyro quickly becomes an efficient boat handler. But there are times when concentration wavers, for instance when you are nearing the end of the almost-joined-together thirty-seven locks approaching the summit of the Bourgogne.

It will be necessary to make drain holes in the 'bottoms' of the tyres. I have sometimes been advised to cover my tyres so that black smudges do not rub off on other people's topsides (and my own). Flour sacks have been recommended. But in my experience the covering soon gets dirty too, so that topsides are not protected by this method. If we are going alongside a yacht we use our white fenders; alongside anything else we use tyres but an additional and useful safeguard we now employ is to drape over the topsides a thick plastic sheet, securing it to the stanchions. This has proved to be most satisfactory on a number of our inland waterway cruises and on reaching the sea we simply discard it.

A plank or two comes in very useful for hanging outside of the tyres when alongside pontoons or piles that otherwise work their way inside of the protective tyres and make contact with the hull. The plank is sure to come in handy doubling up as a gangplank when, for some reason, there is too big a gap between the boat and the shore. A hole in each end of the plank will make for easy attachment.

Sometimes it is desirable to come alongside an unscalable quay wall, to have a ladder onboard then makes all the difference between getting ashore and not.

As big a boathook as you can conveniently stow on deck is recommended; if you are a congenital boathook loser, take two. If you have only one, 'find' a long pole on the canal bank as soon as you can. Lock-keepers in the country sections invariably have a fine selection. You will need the pole for fending off, not only from the walls of locks with sloping sides, but from canal banks when you secure in just sufficient depth of water. You see barges moored in this way with poles almost big enough to do duty carrying telephone wires.

You will need two stakes, preferably of metal; these you will find useful, necessary even, to hammer into the bank alongside when there is no other attachment for your warps. And, of course, you will also need a mallet or large hammer for banging the stakes into the ground.

A good searchlight with a wide beam will be essential for the tunnels. In most tunnels you can be towed if you have no searchlight, or if the light you have is considered unsatisfactory. You can, of course, choose to be towed anyhow. Towing times and charges are available at the lock nearest the entrance.

I have read accounts of people who have towed dinghies through the inland waterways, and I cannot imagine anything so calculated to cause anxiety. Sometimes in entering locks there is only just enough room for you to squeeze your boat in, and in such circumstances a dinghy towed astern would certainly be in danger of being crushed between the lock gates. Passing on narrow waterways would be made much more difficult if allowance had to be made for a dinghy weaving about astern on the wash from the barge and the return wash from the bank. You never, never see a barge or other commercial craft towing a dinghy on the inland waterways for this reason. Yet one must have a dinghy and it must be capable of being stowed inboard out of the way. For two reasons I have come to the conclusion over the years that an inflatable is the answer. At sea we keep our inflatable on the foredeck fully inflated; in the event of having to 'take to the boats' we know that there is sufficient buoyancy to support us. We feel particularly strongly about this, having had a wooden dinghy sink under us; and if my wife and I had not been able to swim our cruising days would have ended.

The next advantage of an inflatable is that when we enter the inland waterways we are able to stow it in its bag and put it out of the way.

Warps have a hard working life on the waterways and I consider that four 15 fathom $1\frac{1}{2}$ in to 2 in warps are the minimum that should be carried on an average cruiser of around 8 tons. Every lock puts a strain on them that they do not experience in harbour. The water surges to or from the lock and I watch the warps straining, sometimes chafing over the edge of a lock wall, finding sharp cracks and crevices. Warps are your waterway friends and you should look after them most attentively.

As far as flags are concerned, a French courtesy flag will be needed, of course, and a Q. You might be glad of international code flag G if you find yourself in need of a pilot; in the waterways you would step ashore and find one.

You will need a hooter or siren to warn of your approach. In the peace of the country locks you could almost shout to announce your arrival, but in the commercial sections and harbours, with noise all around, you need something fairly drastic. We have a compressed air siren with a renewable container. Although no bigger than a cocoa tin, it lets off such a blast that I sometimes feel self-conscious about using it. But it works.

Two or three good torches are necessary, for you will often be returning to your boat at night, perhaps on unlighted canal banks. Replacement batteries and torches are easy enough to buy anywhere in France.

The only other necessary items that might be classed as deck equipment are portable containers for fuel, water, and paraffin, as many as you can stow. There are so many different shapes and sizes of plastic container that it is well worth going to the trouble of finding ones that fit your available stowage space; you will also need filling funnels for each. Hose is hardly worth the space it takes up, for it never seems to be of the right fitting or length. Wherever there is a lock-side water tap you can be fairly certain that there will be a hose attached to it. This may be the moment to suggest that your filler caps should be attached inboard by a wire or line.

Sailing yachts will need planned-in-advance stowage on deck for the mast when it is unstepped. Trestles at each end of the boat are simplest, with the centre of the mast resting on the top of the coachroof, in the tabernacle if there is a convenient one. Pieces of foam rubber are useful for protecting the masts at points of contact and at each end if there is an overhang. I am often asked if the overhang of masts presents a problem in going through the waterways. I have just (August 1981) taken a boat through with an overhang of 8ft at each end and I would say that this is about the limit one should contemplate. The difficulty arises in the smaller locks when you are below the level of the lock wall, and the rush of water causes the boat to swing strongly. Stationing oneself right forward with a boathook at the ready is the answer but it can be a bit of a strain at times.

A supply of strong, stringed labels should be taken to label separately each item of standing and running rigging, blocks and shackles before the mast is unstepped; as soon as it is laid on the deck the shambles of rigging will resemble a fallen tree. A few spare mast bolts are worth taking in case a replacement is needed.

Masts can be left at the yacht compound in the Petit Port at Le Havre (where it is convenient to unstep it), and stepped on return. This is by far the best idea for any sailing yacht intending to stay in the inland waterways, for the mast and rigging are always in the way on deck and the overhang of the mast can be a nuisance as already mentioned. Regular visitors to the inland waterways would be best suited with a motor cruiser.

Below deck, an inland waterway cruise calls for no special equipment. Bottled gas fittings in France are readily interchangeable with equipment supplied in the U.K. thanks to an adaptor that you can buy at any chandler or caravan store. The U.K. Calor bottles are not available in France where you use the Gaz containers widely available in shops and supermarkets. Empty Calor cylinders would be non-fare-paying passengers so plan accordingly.

If you happen to have paraffin appliances onboard you will find that paraffin is widely available under the name of *Pétrole Supérieur*, from *Peintures, Drogueries*. Methylated spirit is obtainable from the same source, also from some food stores, and is known as *Alcool à Brûler*.

It is a good idea to have fire extinguishers strategically sited.

Refrigerators are a blessing and the usual objection to them in boats—that they drain the batteries—does not apply to inland waterway cruising. The engine is in use sufficiently to keep the batteries fully charged. Most boat fridges operate from electricity or gas but electricity is the choice in the waterways.

7 Planning the Cruise

Having decided upon your boat, the next step is to plan your cruise through the French canals.

The limits of your cruise will obviously depend upon the time that you have available and whether, in this time, you propose a return trip or a one-way trip, leaving your boat in France ready for your next cruising adventure (in which case you would either return by train or, more conveniently, in a hire-it-here-leave-it-there hire car, see **Hire Cars**).

Even if you have unlimited time you are not allowed to cruise in your boat in France for more than six months at a time unless, after this time, you are willing to be liable for payment of import duty on the value of your boat; but if your boat is not being used in France you can surrender your ship's papers to the French Customs and leave it there without this time reckoning against your six months' allowance. Many people do this, leaving their boat at some convenient spot in France until the 'next time'.

If you wish to use your boat in France for money-making purposes (such as charter), you will be liable for French T.V.A. from the date of arrival.

The *Permis de Circulation* is no longer required. The only sort of boat needing advance documentation is a boat towed on a car trailer; for this type of craft the necessary triptyque will be issued by the A.A. or R.A.C.

You should apply to the French Government Tourist Office, 178 Piccadilly, London, W.1., for the current list of *chomages*, which shows which locks are closed for maintenance work and when; this maintenance work usually extends throughout the summer months.

In addition to these lock closures for fixed repair periods some lock sections are closed on Sundays, some on Wednesdays. The first lock in any section will usually have the appropriate notice.

The following few extracts from a typical list of *chomages* will

illustrate the necessity of consulting the current list before you plan
your cruise:

Canal de Calais   Écluse d'Henuin (closed for 7 days from 22 June to 29 June)

anal de la Somme   Écluses de Frise supérieure, de Froissy, de Montière et de Pont-Rémy (closed for 30 days from 20 June to 20 July)

Rivière de Marne
(a) De l'écluse de Vandières à celle d'Azy (closed for 21 days from 1 to 22 July)
(b) De l'écluse de Charly à celle de Lesches (closed for 21 days from 1 to 22 July)
(c) De l'écluse de Lesches à celle de Neuilly sur Marne (closed for 15 days from 1 to 16 July)

anal de la Marne au Rhin
(a) De Vitry-le-François à Troussey (closed for 15 days from 7 to 22 July)
(b) De Dombasle au bief de partage de Réchicourt aux petites portes du Lindres (closed for 15 days from 10 to 25 July)

Canal de Bourgogne   De Pont-Royal à St. Jean-de-Losne (closed for 30 days from 19 May to 18 June)

Canal du Nivernais
(a) De l'écluse de Loire No. 35 a Cercy de la Tour (closed for 21 days from 9 to 30 August)
(b) De Cercy la Tour à Sardy (closed for 26 days from 1 to 27 April)
(c) De Sardy à Auxerre (closed for 20 days from 19 May to 8 June)

Rivière d'Yonne
(a) D'Auxerre à Villevallier (closed for 22 days from 19 May to 10 June)
(b) De Villevallier à Port-Renard (closed for 17 days from 22 May to 8 June)
(c) De Port-Renard à Cannes (closed for 10 days from 22 May to 1 June)

These are a few examples from a list of sixty, but they will serve to illustrate the necessity of consulting the list of *chomages* before you plan your tour. A new list is available in March each year from the French Government Tourist Office.

A *Certificat de Capacité* is a certificate of ability testifying to the holder's competence to handle a boat, and is not necessary for yachts under 20 tons.

You will obviously need to check that all passports are up to date. You should complete British Customs Form C.1328 before leaving the U.K. for France. Part 1 of this triplicate form should be deposited with your nearest Customs Office; Parts 2 and 3 should be carried aboard and Part 2 should be handed in when clearing Customs on returning to the U.K. The *passeport du navire étranger* which used to be issued by the French Customs (*Douane*) on entering France has been discontinued; but you still report to French Customs if you wish to buy 'duty frees'.

Whilst dealing with the official documents required you will be planning your route, using the route map in conjunction with the route details and the appropriate Michelin map shown, noting the names of the towns that lie on or near the route of your proposed cruise. As already mentioned, the *Syndicat d'Initiative* at these towns will be pleased to send you details of items of interest or of any special event planned for the time that you will be there.

2 (opposite) and 3. Very occasionally plans can go astray, as in May–June 1973, for instance, when the *batelier* went on strike and blocked the Seine at Rouen. Many yachts failed to get past the *batelier barrier* but many more were allowed through, some several times. Demands to pass, reminiscent of gunboat diplomacy, failed to open the strikers' hearts or barriers; charm, as ever, succeeded. The centre barges formed a 'gate', as shown above.

Waterway maps of France are available from: Les éditions du plaisancier, B.P.27/69641, Caluire, France. 1, Carte de France 32F; 2, Guide du Doubs 51F; 3, Guide du Rhône 56F.

If you are going to need help with the channel crossing to France it will also be necessary to arrange this with an experienced friend. You will obviously want the appropriate charts; your compass and other navigational aids should be checked so that you will be suitably prepared on the great day.

8 In the Waterways of France

On arrival at your French port of entry you will be flying your Q flag (and your French courtesy flag) and you will keep your Q flying until you have been cleared by customs. You are more likely to find them than they are to find you. The owner, or a member of the crew delegated by him, should take to the Customs (*Douane*) the passports of each person on board, also a list of their names and the ship's papers. It has already been explained that the issue of the *passeport du navire étranger* has been discontinued; also that British yachts entering France must be British Registered as from 1 January 1984. (I have always felt happier when cruising into France to have as a visiting card for my yacht a British Certificate of Registry, and of the nine yachts I have owned all have been British Registered.) If the Customs House is closed when you call you must keep your Q flag flying until you are cleared. So long as you land no dutiable goods it will be perfectly in order to go ashore before Customs formalities have been completed.

Not everyone bothers to take passports and a list of persons on board to the *Commissariat des Renseignements Généraux* (Immigration Office), but it is a rule that it should be done before visiting the Customs.

If your boat has a mast it will be necessary to unstep it, and facilities for this exist at all entry ports; there will also be fuel and water available, and it will be a sensible precaution to top up before setting off.

It will be an exciting moment when you set off on your inland cruise. If this happens to be a busy commercial waterway like the Seine, you will have plenty of interesting company of all shapes and sizes.

At first, until you get accustomed to it, the river traffic ahead will appear to be scattered all over your line of approach but, as in

4.   Plenty of company . . .

5.   . . . of all shapes and sizes. Over 300 cars on a 'Pusher' barge.

life, when you get up to them you will find that the problems will
have miraculously disappeared.

The rule of the road is, of course, to keep to the right. When you
get on to the shallower sections there is an exception to this rule; a
heavily laden barge will have to follow the deep water channel
whichever side of the waterway this takes him. If he comes over to
'your side' he will put out from the starboard side of his wheelhouse a large blue flag and you then alter course to pass him on his
blue flag side. Not all pleasure craft bother to acknowledge the
signal, but if you wish to do so you should equip yourself with a
blue flag about 60 × 90cm on a stick about 1,50m long.

Whilst on the subject of passing it may be the moment to explain
that when, later on, you come to the narrower canals you must slow
down on meeting an oncoming barge and inch your way in towards

6. You will be the overtaken vessel.

the bank on your side as far as you dare. As his bow wave
approaches you increase your speed and again when you are
amidships of him, aiming back into the centre of the channel
through the wash of his screw.

Occasionally in the canals you may come across barges pulled
by tractors or animals and it will obviously be necessary to pass on
the side opposite to the tow.

Right from the start you should keep a good look out for
dredgers. They are usually held in their dredging position by a line
to the bank and will be exhibiting a signal showing which side to

pass. A green circle with a white centre shows the side to pass; a white circle with a red centre shows the side not to pass. Sometimes dredgers are secured by lines to both banks and they will lower one of them into the water on your approach; but it is as well to look through the binoculars to be sure that they have seen you, not that your siren will be of much avail to announce your approach, for it would take an atomic explosion to compete with the racket of the dredging buckets.

If you see a barge displaying a red flag amidships it is an indication that he is turning in that direction and should not be overtaken on that side.

It is likely that you will be the overtaken vessel most of the time, particularly on the wide waterways, and you will be overtaken without comment, just as you will overtake the odd slower craft that you come up on. Some yachts fit a rear mirror so that they can see what is coming up astern without turning round, but you do not really need this eye in the back of your head to the extent that you do in a car; boats and ships move relatively so much slower, and since it is likely that you will be constantly interested to look all around you it will be a rare occasion that a craft will creep up on you unobserved. If you are in the way you will hear about it. If you

7.   Difficult to pass—on the Marne . . .

keep well over to your side of the channel you will not attract attention.

In the narrower waterways where there is just room to pass, one is supposed to signal a request to overtake by hooting one long and one short if it is desired to pass to starboard and one long and two short if it is desired to pass to port. The answering signal to pass is one short to starboard and two short to port; four short means a refusal to let the overtaking vessel pass. This should not be construed as an outburst of bloody-mindedness, but simply that the skipper ahead can see a hazard that has not come into the view of the overtaking craft.

On some of the narrower canals, if you come up behind a barge going your way it is not likely that you will be able to pass him however much you toot. At each lock he will get ahead temporarily while the lock chamber is being refilled or re-emptied for you. It is foolish to allow yourself to become frustrated at being continually held up in this way. Far better to stop at some pleasant spot for sightseeing or shopping and thus allow the barge to get clear ahead. It may be that, by waiting, you will allow for the possibility of a barge coming from the opposite direction; then you will have all the locks 'set up' ready for you to enter (except in a few sections

8.   . . . and on the Canal du Rhône au Rhin.

where the lock gates are always put one way after traffic has passed).

In case it may be wondered how barges going opposite ways can pass if it is impossible to pass when going the same way, the answer is that they squeeze past somehow. It takes so much longer to pass a barge when going the same way. You cannot blame him for keeping going, and it is a hair raising experience to try to squeeze slowly by over his stern and bow wave with only inches to spare.

When approaching bridges with a number of arches you will see signals on the bridges showing you which channel to take, as follows:

2 red horizontal bars with a white stripe between	**No Entry** from the direction you are coming from
1 yellow diamond	Two-way traffic
2 yellow diamonds	**Entry** from your direction only (one-way traffic)

In the canals there are many narrow sections underneath bridges, and you will need to be ready to 'put your brakes on' urgently if a barge suddenly appears from round the corner ahead as you approach. Never attempt a race to the opening, for it is

9. Narrow sections under bridges.

likely that you will be able to stop much quicker than the opposition. In going astern, as you will have to, be sure to go astern far enough, for the barge will sometimes clear the opening with maddening slowness; if you have gone ahead too soon it is an alarming experience to have the barge alongside you and no room ahead.

In fact, these encounters with barges are very rarely met, for it is usual to cruise all day long on the smaller canals without seeing more than two or three. But when you do meet them it is as well to be prepared.

Where 'traffic lights' are positioned at bridges, tunnels, locks, etc., the signal is:

Red   Stop

Green   Go

Red and Green   Stand by

The channel that you are to follow is usually obvious, but not always so. The entrance to a lock might turn off quietly left or right, leaving what appears to be a splendid waterway ahead . . . until you observe the spray haze rising up from the falling water of a weir. Near towns there are sometimes bridges busy with traffic that holds your attention, until it is diverted by a local citizen on

10.   Avoid tying up near to locks.

the nearby bank afflicted, apparently, with St. Vitus's Dance; you realize that he is only trying to attract your attention to dangers ahead. Going back you find that you missed the proper turning.

Although you can tie up anywhere you should avoid doing so near to locks because barges will want to wait, or pass, here and it is likely that they will be up earlier than you in the morning. No traffic moves on the majority of French waterways at night and it is a delight to tie up to trees, by some grassy bank, in the certain knowledge that your sleep is not going to be disturbed.

I have heard 'bargees' (*bateliers*) and lock-keepers criticized as being unhelpful and unkind to yachtsmen, but I have never had this experience. Some people have a facility for rubbing everyone up the wrong way and they complain when the effect of their attitude rebounds on them. In life generally, scowls are traded for scowls and smiles for smiles; the French canals are no exception.

Go through the inland waterways determined to have an enjoyable cruise and everyone you meet will help you to achieve it.

9 Locks

TIMES OF OPENING

1 to 15 October	6.30 am to 6.30 pm
16 to 31 October	7.00 am to 6.00 pm
I November to 31 January	7.30 am to 5.30 pm
February	7.30 am to 6.30 pm
1 to 15 March	7.00 am to 7.00 pm
16 March to 30 September	6.30 am to 7.30 pm

(Only a few waterways are worked all night)

Many people, women particularly, have told me that what puts them off an inland waterway cruise is a fear of locks. They can rest assured that there is no justification for this at all; it is certainly a fear that vanishes after one or two locks have been successfully negotiated.

A certain competence in handling a boat is necessary in order to make the trip at all, and no special skill is needed to go in and out of locks. As for being worried about locks simply because of their size, the biggest of all, the Bollène, raises or lowers you in its 25m cathedral-like chamber without a ripple. By comparison, a lock-keeper 'cowboy' (rare indeed), can cause discomfort by changing a 1,50m level too quickly if you are not secured properly.

Locks vary in size and operation according to the traffic carried. Some locks have a gate in the centre, so that it can be a half-size or a full-size lock according to the traffic. Busy waterway sections have big locks, often automatically operated. The quieter country sections have small single locks, manually operated by the lock-keeper or, more usually, by his wife assisted by a crew member of the boat passing through. This should be looked upon as the splendid exercise that it is, and it is a pity that some of the lock-keeping ladies do not have waist-lines to recommend it.

Entering the French waterways from England, the commercial size locks will be the first to be encountered, and it may therefore be as well to consider the big locks first; also ascending locks, since these will need to be dealt with before the descending.

Imagine that you are approaching your first lock.

Barges will be waiting their turn to enter, quite often more barges than the lock will accommodate; some barges will be secured to the bank, others drifting in the waterway, others coming up fast astern.

All will be leaving a way clear for the 'other way' barges to come out of the lock (we are assuming that our first lock is filling from the opposite direction as we approach).

The invariable rule for pleasure craft is to keep out of the way of all commercial craft, displaying to them 'after you' politeness which they will appreciate all the more since they have to pay for using their waterways and you do not.

Seek no preference over a barge because you arrived at the lock before him.

At the same time, try to satisfy yourself that the waiting barges are, in fact, waiting for the lock and not just waiting. In some of the industrial areas, barges, three and four deep, secure to quays waiting for work. These quays may be just before a lock, and you would have a long wait if you decided to defer to some of them. Even barges that you are following may decide to 'park'. If you have any doubt about such a situation always enquire, in French or sign language, by going alongside the nearest occupied barge. In a wide waterway there can be no harm in going ahead to have a look at the lock, returning to a suitable station having done so. In a narrow waterway this will not be wise as the waiting barges may be queuing to enter a one-way section or traffic-light-controlled tunnel.

If you can see the lock ahead you will be able to judge how long you will have to wait to enter. Barges in the lock going your way will mean a long wait; or if the lock is just filling with barges from the opposite direction it will be best for you to secure.

Do not assume that because a barge is secured to the bank there will be sufficient water for you alongside the bank unless the barge is deeply laden.

In any case it will usually be more convenient for you to go alongside a barge that is tied up to the bank; if the *batelier* is in view, a raised warp and eyebrow accompanied by a smile will be sufficient to obtain his approval. If he is not in view simply secure to the bitts on his deck. Your crew will have a warp ready to loop over the bitts, and the *batelier* may even help you to secure. This is an occasion when your stock of sweets (brought specially for the purpose) will be brought out if you see any children on the barge.

Secure to the barge in such a manner that you can instantly cast off. Keep a lookout for any new arrival coming up astern and vacate your place alongside if there appears to be nowhere else for the newcomer to secure, particularly if he is a big or double barge.

These gestures are noted and appreciated; some of the barges waiting in your company at this lock may be in your company for the rest of the day through other locks when you may need them.

When the lock opens, the 'other way' traffic will come streaming out. If the waterway is wide enough for you to stay well clear of this oncoming traffic do so; in narrow waterways remain secured to the bank fore and aft until it has passed or it will suck you in towards it as it goes by. As soon as it has all passed by, let go and move out of the way of the barges going in. Stay to one side as near to the lock as convenient.

The lock-keeper's directions will echo over the water from his loudspeaker, but do not be concerned if you cannot understand what he is saying. It is unlikely that a pleasure craft would be

11. 'Other Way' traffic will come streaming out.

12.   Some locks are operated . . .

directed into the lock first so you will have time to watch the barges.

The barges move forward as directed, and where directed if the lock has more than one chamber, tucking themselves in alongside each other. As the lock space is taken up you stand up nearer, out of the way to one side, ready to move ahead. 'After you' politeness is not discarded but the time approaches when barges waiting with you will not be able to get into the space left and you will.

At this time it may be that the loudspeaker will call you forward; it may be that you will not understand what the loudspeaker voice is saying. It is then likely that from the waiting barges (impressed by your politeness) will appear much shouting and waving urging you forward.

If there is no loudspeaker it is simply a question of judging when no more barges can be taken in but you can; or perhaps the last barge is seen thrashing astern, unable to squeeze in.

You move ahead smartly; one lock gate will probably be closing as you approach, perhaps both. As you prepare to nose inside, a lock-keeper may indicate where he wants you to lie but, more probably, there will be only one obvious space available.

Your foredeck hand (your wife) should have a coiled rope in hand ready to throw in case the lock-keeper shows any interest in receiving it and assuming that he is near. It is probable that he will be if the lock gates are manually operated. Some of the bigger locks and all of the huge ones are operated by the remote control of a

... from
control
towers.

lock-keeper in a control tower. The really big locks have vast steel
shutters that rise up and down instead of gates.

The lock sides will be too high for you to climb. It is not likely
that there will be iron rungs set in the lock wall just where you are.
If the lock-keeper holds out his hand for your warp he will
appreciate receiving it accurately thrown, first time. When ropes
have become soggy bundles of knitting that fall short of the lock-
keeper's outstretched hand he is liable to walk away. If he receives
your line he will take it round a bollard (out of your vision since
you are 'down below') and throw the end back down to you if it is
long enough.

If the lock-keeper does not appear to take your line you secure to
a barge; in the space left for you it may not be a question of selecting one, for the last in will be the only one that you can get at to
secure.

His decks may be cleaner than yours so try not to dirty them;
his sides most certainly will not be, so have your tyres out over the
side as protection.

14. Secured to a barge in a lock only half full of barges.

Whilst securing, keep your eye on the lock gates closing behind you to make sure that your stern has not drifted back into them.

Soon after the gates close, the water level will begin to rise. If you are secured to one of the lock bollards you must take up on your rope as you rise, to keep your station; secured to a barge you have no worry in this respect.

As you rise up above the lock wall it is wise to detach, if you are secured to a barge, and push off to secure to a bollard on the lock. All the barges in the lock will be getting ready to move out as soon as the gates ahead open; when their screws start turning you will need to be secured. The swirling water will create no problem if you are tied to a bollard.

Allow all the barges to go on ahead before you let go. You may see them tossing something to the lock-keeper (stationed judiciously) as they leave. It is not necessary for a pleasure craft to consider tipping unless some very special service has been rendered.

Having successfully negotiated your first lock you realize that there was nothing to worry about after all.

In very deep, large, locks there are set in the lock walls, movable bollards that slide up and down with you so that there is no need to adjust your ropes as the water level changes. Or sometimes, in

15. Movable bollards slide up and down the walls in deep locks.

smaller locks, the lock-keeper of a deep lock will reach down a long pole with a hook on the end to take your warp. Some yachts carry such poles, with hooks on the end, for passing warps to lock-keepers and for reaching around bollards.

Not all locks have straight sides; where they are sloping, 'V' shaped, it is slightly more difficult to get a line ashore, and instead of trying to do so it will be easier to secure to a barge if one is available. (Some locks have one side sloping and one straight.)

16. Lock with sloping sides.

17.   Made to measure.

However, small locks will be the ones most frequently encountered. Since they fit like a glove the type of barge using them, there
is no question of sharing these locks with a barge. See the illustra-
tion showing how snugly the barge Malvine fits into the lock; 'made
for it' one might say, as indeed the barges are. Incidentally, the
little lady 'driver' of Malvine is an object lesson in relaxed control
as she manoeuvres her huge charge through the lock.

The smaller locks are on the waterways with little traffic, and it

18. An object
lesson . . .

19. . . . in relaxed
control.

is usual to go for a whole day without meeting more than two or three barges.

Two or three yachts can be accommodated in the smaller locks, and the lock routine can then be shared between crews.

On approaching a small lock, if the gates are closed against you and no one is in view, a toot on your siren/hooter will usually bring someone from the lock house to start opening one gate for you. Whether anyone appears or not, nose your craft into the bank and put a crew member ashore, to find the lock-keeper, if necessary, and to open the other gate. If the beam of your boat allows of your entering through one opened gate, your crew member will go up the lock ladder once inside.

Should it be lunch time, this will be the moment to have your own lunch, too. Many lock-keepers like to have their lunch undisturbed, and who can blame them?

Obviously the gates will not be opened for you until the water in the lock chamber is equalized to your level.

If, on approaching, the lock gates are open, look to see whether the iron rung ladder is set in the right or left wall. They are situated fairly constantly, all right or all left, for long sections of locks at a time, and only appear to change when you get too confident in your anticipation.

20. Lock open in your favour.

21. Winding up the sluice handles . . .

22. . . . to let the
water in.

23. Circular lock. It is impossible to keep all of the boat alongside. Watch for
occasional sluices causing cross currents.

Nose your craft up to the ladder so that your crew can step off
on to it carrying a suitable length of attached (to the boat) bow
warp coiled over her (his?) shoulder like a mountain climber. The
crew should get into the habit of gaining the quay quickly and
allowing for the pull on the warp once the boat starts moving into
the lock. Move on into the lock, the crew will take a turn round a
bollard and throw the end of the warp back down to you. If your
crew is already ashore to open the gate you will need to have your
warp ready coiled to throw and to stand by for its return. Secure aft
and be ready to take up as the water rises.

The lock-keeper will close one gate behind you, and if the
second gate has been opened your crew will close that. They will
then walk up to the gates ahead and wind up the sluice handles to
let the water in.

When the lock water level is equalized, the lock-keeper and your
crew will wind open the forward gates, you toss your warp from the
bollard (having taken up on it the whole time that the water was
coming into the lock), your crew steps on board, and you wave
goodbye to the lock-keeper.

There are many different types of locks: large, small, straight-
sided, sloping, rectangular, circular, but they all follow the same
pattern in the same waterway section.

Staircase locks are a series of locks joined together, the inside
lock gates of the first lock chamber being the outside lock gates of

24. Looking down a flight of seven staircase locks.

25. The gate ahead becomes the gate behind as you move forward.

the next and so on. When you are going through staircase locks, having put your crew ashore at the first one as already described, you move out of one lock into the next one, your crew remaining ashore to carry your warp up (or down) the staircase.

In cases where there are no facilities to put your crew ashore and there appears to be special difficulty in getting a warp ashore without help, it will invariably be found that the necessary help is readily available to greet you. It is sometimes easy to forget that one is not the first to pass that way.

So far, the procedure for ascending has been outlined. Descending is easier in that you enter the lock at quay level and can reach out to loop your warp over a bollard. But if, on approach, the gates are closed against you it will still be appreciated (by the lock-keeper) if you put your crew ashore to open the second gate should your boat be unable to fit through the space left by the gate opened by the lock-keeper. (Incidentally, whether ascending or descending, if you do not put crew ashore to help the lock-keeper he will,

26.   Crew waiting to rejoin after lock 'duty'.

of course, do it all himself—in time.)

Your crew and the lock-keeper walk ahead to the forward gates to open the sluices. It is now of the utmost importance to ensure that your warp is not secured both ends on board. If they are, the rope will tighten up as you are lowered in the lock, the deck fitting to which it is attached will be pulled out; or the rope will break; or your boat will be left hanging on the lock wall.

But I am sorry to say that this happens to the best of us; in fact it is easy enough to be diverted at that vital moment when the level of water is going down in the lock chamber and your warp is coming up taut. Kettles always whistle at such moments, and you just pop into the cabin to turn the heat off; or you may be searching in the cabin for something that a comment by the lock-keeper has brought to your mind.

Your turn round your cleat may be impossible to undo when it comes under considerable strain. If you are faced with this situation, shout immediately to have the sluices closed; it may then be necessary to let in some water again (from the other end of the lock, of course) to take off the strain and get your warp free.

Locks with sloping sides obviously need a special routine, for when descending in them your hull will quickly make contact with the sloping lock wall. If you have bilge keels they will be caught in the uneven stonework of the wall and your boat will heel over as the water level falls away. Should this happen you must again shout for the sluices to be closed; if you then cannot push yourself free, the lock must be refilled until you can.

A simple routine to avoid these problems in descending sloping locks is to position yourself amidships holding the boat-hook and/or a long pole to push your boat away from the lock wall as you descend. You will need to have the free end of your warp in your hand as well, gently pulling on the warp (which will be around a bollard ashore) and pushing on the boat-hook to maintain position. If you have sufficient crew to 'pole off' at either end of the boat, so much the better.

Another point to watch in descending is that you are far enough forward in the lock (away from the gates you have entered) to avoid the possibility of your rudder lodging on the shelf or step just inside the lock.

When you are down to the required water level your warp is pulled back on board; for this reason the warp is passed round the bollard and not tied to it.

Whether in sloping or straight-sided locks you are now 'low

27.   Variety and interest. From a country lock to . . .

28.   (opposite) . . . the Bollène

down' and your crew is 'high up' ashore. If there are iron rungs set
in the lock wall your crew will come down them to you. Sometimes,
in place of rungs in the lock wall, there are steps at the end of the
lock, and your crew can rejoin the boat from there.

In ascending locks the chamber will obviously be filled by water
flowing in from ahead of you and often a bow warp only would
suffice to secure you; in descending locks, with the flow going past
from astern of you, a stern warp would often suffice. But it is wise
to make a habit of securing fore and aft at all times; a single warp
around one bollard ashore will do. You will then be safeguarded
against swirls and eddies. If you swing out of line look to your
helm. Your boat will steer in the moving water filling or emptying
the lock and the position of your rudder is clearly of great
importance.

If you look upon locks as an irksome chore you will not enjoy the
inland waterways of France. Make up your mind to enjoy their
variety and interest and your cruise will be one of the most
worthwhile experiences of your life.

10 Cost of Living, Shopping and Stores

At the present rate of exchange you can reckon on a franc being worth about 10p.

Living is no dearer in France than it is in England at the present time and the choice and arrangement of French food for sale generally has always been preferred by a lot of people. Shopping in France should be a joyful experience and I feel sorry for those so 'dul of soul' that they find it a bore.

Most holidaymakers are obliged to eat out which is obviously more expensive than eating at home; but the yachtsman in France has with him his cruising home so that he can appreciate the delight of French shops, supermarkets and open markets.

The coffee and snack habit is expensive in any country. You get the best selection of *prix fixe* meals in France, also they will be beautifully presented and served long after the 'chef's gone home' time in Britain.

It should be obvious that bacon and eggs for breakfast are as relatively expensive in France as *croissants* are in England. Holiday-makers who insist upon continuing English eating habits when abroad are usually the loudest to complain about the cost of living.

When people are so insistent that the cost of living is prohibitive in France I can never understand how they imagine that the working classes there live; for the average wage there is not very high and yet one sees very few bodies lying around on the pavements in an emaciated condition. For myself, I do not complain about the cost of butter in a country where one can buy a bottle of *Appellation Contrôlée* wine for 8op.

Every town and village seems to have its charming little market where fresh vegetables, eggs, and chickens are brought in fresh from the country and cost no more than they do in the U.K., if as much. The chickens are not always dressed it is true, but the courage needed to undertake this rather distasteful chore is available in a beautiful variety of bottles; sometimes your purchase is handed to you alive, trussed by the feet, in which case you will have a most interesting cycle ride in getting it back to the boat. And once on board it is likely that your meal will be long deferred.

Lock-keepers in the country sections sometimes have eggs and vegetables to sell. Often there are a variety of shops near locks. The most constant shopping need is for bread and milk, of course, which costs much the same as it does in the U.K.

A large tin of milk powder should always be carried for emergencies. In fact you can keep your cost of living down in France by taking with you as many canned foods as your storage space will hold. Meat is relatively dear in France, so why not take with you a large selection of canned varieties; sausages, as we know them, are virtually unobtainable, so that if you are partial to the good old English 'banger' you should take what you can with you. Butter is dear, but can you tell margarine from butter? Jams and marmalades are also expensive in France, so that your stores should include these also 'café size' tins of coffee and milk drinks and a really large box of tea bags. You cannot buy the bacon that you are accustomed to in England, but will probably prefer to eat a French breakfast when in France. Although there are hundreds of different cheeses made in France, few of them are cheap.

You can buy bread every day including Sundays and holidays; if one *boulangerie* is closed it is likely that there will be another one open nearby.

A longish lunch period is usual for all shops, but they stay open until quite late in the evening. Many shops close on Mondays, but the village store type of shop seems to be open for long hours every day and often on Sundays and holidays.

The main item of shopping for your boat will be fuel. Petrol costs more than diesel fuel in France.

Wherever there are cars and trucks there will always be fuel stations somewhere, but if you allow your fuel tanks to run low that will surely be the time when you are a long way from a fuel station. It is a good habit to keep your fuel tanks topped up whenever you see fuel pumps by the waterway. If you decide to take a bicycle it will provide wheels for your heavy fuel loads. Before carrying fuel in cans, however, it is as well to enquire if there is a local fuel delivery service.

SHOPPING VOCABULARY

apple—*pomme*
apricot—*abricot*
artichoke—*artichaut*
asparagus—*asperges*
bacon—*lard*
baker—*boulangerie*
banana—*banane*
beef—*boeuf*
beefsteak—*bifteck*
  (well done—*bien cuit*;
  medium—*à point*;
  rare—*saignant*)
beer—*bière*
beetroot—*betterave*
blackcurrant—*cassis*
bread—*pain*
broccoli—*brocoli*
Brussels sprouts—*choux*
  de Bruxelles
butcher—*boucherie*
butter—*beurre*
cabbage—*chou*
can opener—*ouvre-boîte*
carrot—*carrotte*
cauliflower—*choufleur*
celery—*céleri*
cheese—*fromage*
chemist—*pharmacie*
cherries—*cerises*
chicken—*poulet*
chop—*côte*
cocoa—*cacao*
cod—*morue*
coffee—*café*
confectioners—*confiserie*
crab—*crabe*
cream—*crème*
cucumber—*concombre*
cutlets—*côtelettes*
duck—*canard*
egg—*oeuf*
figs—*figues*
fish—*poisson*

fishmonger—*poissonnerie*
flour—*farine*
French beans—*haricots*
  verts
frogs—*grenouilles*
fruit—*fruit*
fruit shop—*fruiterie*
grape—*raisin*
grapefruit—*pample-*
  mousse
grocer—*épicerie*
haddock—*eglefin*
hake—*colin*
halibut—*flétan*
ham—*jambon*
herring—*hareng*
honey—*miel*
ice—*glace*
jam—*confiture*
kidney beans—*flageolets*
kidneys—*rognons*
lamb—*agneau*
lark—*alouette*
lemon—*citron*
lettuce—*laitue*
liver—*foie* (beef liver—
  foie de boeuf; calves'
  liver—*foie de veau*;
  lambs' liver—*foie*
  d'agneau)
lobster—*homard*
mackerel—*maquereau*
margarine—*margarine*
marrow—*moelle*
meat—*viande*
milk—*lait*
mushrooms—*champignons*
mussels—*moules*
mustard—*moutarde*
mutton—*mouton*
oil—*huile*
olive—*olive*
onion—*oignon*

orange—*orange*
oysters—*huîtres*
parsnip—*panais*
pastry shop—*pâtisserie*
peach—*pêche*
pear—*poire*
peas—*pois*
pineapple—*ananas*
plaice—*carrelet* or *plie*
plum—*prune*
pork—*porc*
potato—*pomme de terre*
prawns—*bouquets* or
  crevettes
rabbit—*lapin*
raspberry—*framboise*
rhubarb—*rhubarbe*
salmon—*saumon*
salt—*sel*
sausages—*saucissons*
slice—*tranche*
snails—*escargots*
sole—*sole*
soup—*potage*
spaghetti—*spaghetti*
spinach—*épinards*
strawberry—*fraise*
sugar—*sucre*
sweetbreads—*ris de vea*
tart—*tarte*
tea—*thé*
thrush—*grive*
tin—*boîte*
tomato—*tomate*
tripe—*tripes*
trout—*truite*
turbot—*turbot*
turnip—*navets*
veal—*veau*
vinegar—*vinaigre*
water—*eau*

29. Petrol pumps alongside, Auxerre.

Now that F.O.D. (*fuel oil doméstique*) is no longer available to pleasure boat engines it is more than ever necessary to top up tanks at every convenient opportunity and to carry spare cans onboard. The sources from which barges draw their fuel are no longer allowed to supply yachts. Some fuel stations are equipped to supply both and if adjacent to a road, vehicles also. You are, however, allowed to take on F.O.D. if you say that it is for your heating system.

T.V.O. or tractor vapourizing oil is not available in France so it is no good expecting to find supplies.

If you are unfortunate enough to have an engine breakdown you

MECHANICAL VOCABULARY

acid — *acide*
armature — *armature*
battery, to top — *reniveler la batterie*
bolt — *boulon*
carburettor — *carburateur*
choke — *starter*
diesel — *diesel*
diesel fuel — *gas-oil*
dipstick — *réglette-jauge*

distributor — *distributeur*
distributor head — *distributeur de courant*
dynamo — *dynamo*
engine — *moteur*
fill up — *faire le plein*
fuel tank — *réservoir d'essence* (or *gas-oil*)
insulating tape — *chatterton*

jet — *gicleur*
nut — *écrou*
oil — *huile*
petrol — *essence*
screw — *vis*
screwdriver — *tournevis*
self-starter — *démarreur*
spanner, adjustable — *clé à molette*
washer — *rondelle*
water — *eau*

will find that the average French mechanic is quite resourceful in dealing with purely motor departments of your engine; as far as the marine department is concerned there are marine engineers at many of the points where barges gather. To take a kit of spares is a reasonable precaution, for it usually ensures that the parts you have duplicated will keep running satisfactorily.

Paraffin for your cooker and Tilley lamp is known as *pétrole supérieur*, the better kind as *kerdane*. It is available from most *drogueries, peintures*, but there are areas here and there where it is not available so that it is as well to have a number of containers and to keep them topped up. Barges use it, so that it is plentiful in any barge centre. The better type of paraffin costs about a franc a litre, which is quite expensive; if you are able to take supplies it would be wise to do so. There is an inferior kind at half the price, which is sold at many garages; but it may prove to be smokey, although this seems to depend upon the temperament of the paraffin appliance in which it is used.

Methylated spirit is known as *alcool à brûler* and is available at *drogueries* and many food stores at reasonable prices.

Calor Gas fittings are not necessarily interchangeable with Continental Butane Gas fittings, but there is an adapter available to convert Calor Gas fittings for use with Campingaz which is widely available, although rather expensive.

One of the greatest joys, of course, is the cheapness of the best wine in the world and many other drinks. *Vin Ordinaire* seems to be available on draught in supermarkets everywhere. There are many different brands so do not be put off if you do not fancy the first one you try. V.D.Q.S. wines cost from 45p to 60p upwards a bottle and *Appellation Contrôlée* wines from 80p. At these prices you have a wonderful opportunity to experiment.

English and American cigarettes are not particularly cheap in France; if you can develop a taste for the French Gauloises or Gitanes, your smoking bill will be cut dramatically. Pipe tobacco costs less than in the U.K., but cigars are not noticeably cheaper.

There is no charge for being on the waterways. No one comes along to ask you for money for 'parking'. The only exception to this is at the Touring Club de France mooring in Paris. Any yacht club may make a charge for an extended stay, so it is worth finding out the charge on arrival.

The great majority of the locks on the French waterways are free to pleasure craft, but a few locks are privately owned and may make a charge for passing through.

11 Weather and Miscellaneous Items of Interest

Weather Spring and summer are the best times to cruise in the French canals, but some are closed for varying periods from May to September, and the list of chomages should be consulted as already explained. It seems that the experienced French canal-cruising folk prefer to go in April, May, or June. It is well known that all France is on holiday during July and August, not that this means crowded cruising, for the Frenchman is strangely disinterested in using his beautiful waterways; but the holiday crowds would make demands on the facilities ashore. Up to March there is likely to be flooding, when some weirs are opened to navigation and locks are not then used. From September there is likely to be drought; for this latter reason navigation is sometimes impossible in September, October, and November. Therefore, for any proposed cruise outside the months of April to August it would be more than ever necessary to make advance enquiries through the French Government Tourist Office regarding the possibility of completing the journey. Even then, conditions can change from day to day. The seasonal climate of France is not all that much different from our own except, perhaps, for the winter-protected Cote d'Azur. Marseille in December can be as cold as London; and from December, incidentally, the French canals can be ice-bound.

French weather reports can be obtained through the various motoring organizations.

Public holidays in France are: New Year's Day, Easter Monday, 1 May, Ascension Day, Whit Monday, 14 July (Bastille Day), 15 August, 1 November, 11 November, 25 December.

Banks close on these public holidays, also all day on Saturdays (and Sundays, needless to say); on weekdays they are open from 9 am to 4 pm, many closing for an hour or so at lunch time.

Cruising Holidays on the French Waterways

There are many hire cruisers on the inland waterways of France and the popularity of this type of holiday grows every year. In a way—apart from considering the desirability or otherwise of allowing learners on the waterways—it provides proof that you do not need to be an experienced sailor to embark on a voyage of this nature. The owners of such hire craft would not risk their valuable fleets nor would insurers insure them. Obviously it is preferable to have nautical experience to cruise your craft in the inland waterways—and essential to get it there.

Many people write to me asking if I can recommend any particular hire cruiser firm operating in the French waterways. I invariably refer them to current advertising either in the classified columns of the Sunday newspapers or in the yachting press, having found that such cruising data tends to change from year to year.

In addition to the hire cruisers that you 'drive yourself' there are passenger carrying cruise ships, often converted barges, providing luxury travel and sometimes luxury food. We have met them on the Marne, Seine, Yonne and in the Burgundy, Centre, Nivernais,

30.   Canals can be ice-bound from December.

Loing, Briare and Loire Canals. (Such pampered cruising does not prepare for a waterway life in your own boat however.) We have been interested to note that many of the passenger carrying cruise ships have been operated by British owners who have thus discovered an agreeable way of being paid to cruise the inland waterways of France.

Even five years ago, on the Bourgogne, I was told that there were only five hotel barges in the French waterways. Today, I am informed, there are forty. The better ones are fitted out at considerable cost to provide private double cabins with toilet and shower en suite, cordon bleu catering in teak lined dining rooms, deck sun lounges bordered by gay flowers in tubs and gayer umbrellas, and lines of colourful bicycles standing smartly to attention on the foredeck like hands at entering harbour stations. A number of these barges have attendant mini-buses which collect and return you from airport or railway station; the mini-bus also appears at suitable waterway points to whisk guests off to castles or churches, thus sparing them the possibility of becoming bored by their nautical inactivity.

I hear of new ventures of this nature starting up all the time and am sure that there is plenty of scope for everybody. You will probably have noticed that a number of the 'drive yourself' hire cruiser operators are also British.

Another popular hire cruise area is towards the Mediterranean end of the Canal du Midi and also in the Rhône and Petit Rhône, with a brief excursion out into the Sea of Seas on the Languedoc-Roussillon coast. These cruises take you through the waterways of the Camargue, perhaps up to Avignon, to Arles, Aigues-Mortes, Sète and across the étang, the historical richness of the area contrasting vividly with the ultra modern development of the new French shoreline.

There are also shorter trips down the Rhône from Lyon and back (of value to apprehensive skippers waiting anxiously in their craft to venture past the Pierre-Bénite lock).

Hire Cars If you decide to leave your boat in France so that you can continue your cruise when next you have time available, you should surrender your ship's papers to the Customs as already mentioned. If you can make it convenient to leave your boat at a place where 'drive-yourself' hire cars are available, you will be able to bring off your personal gear with the minimum of inconvenience. Hertz and

Avis cars are available at many towns throughout France; wherever you hire them from, you can drive them to Le Havre or any other Channel port and leave them there. You will need an international driving licence which can be obtained from any office of the AA or RAC; you will need a passport-size photograph when applying.

Even if you do not intend to leave your boat in France it may be useful to take an international driving licence with you in case you wish to hire a self-drive car for any reason.

Mail   Can be sent to you c/o Poste Restante at any town and is reliable. A small charge is made on collection of letters.

Telephone   To telephone to the U.K. from France is a simple and automatic business.

Cats and Dogs Cats and dogs can be brought into France provided that they have either:

1. A certificate of origin and health, dated not earlier than three days before the animals' journey, stating that it comes from a country where there has been no epidemic of rabies for three years and that it has spent at least six months in that country, or has been there since birth.

2. A certificate of anti-rabies vaccination stating that the vaccination was given with a vaccine officially administered more than one month and less than six months before entry into France.

Puppies less than three months old and kittens less than six months old may be taken into France upon production of a veterinary certificate confirming age.

ights and Measures

litres	gals	kms	miles	kgs	lbs
1 =	0,22	1 =	0,62	0,453 =	1
2 =	0,44	2 =	1,24	0,907 =	2
3 =	0,66	3 =	1,86	1,360 =	3
4 =	0,88	4 =	2,48	1,814 =	4
5 =	1,10	5 =	3,11	2,268 =	5
6 =	1,32	6 =	3,73	2,721 =	6
7 =	1,54	7 =	4,35	3,175 =	7
8 =	1,76	8 =	4,97	3,628 =	8
9 =	1,98	9 =	5,59	4,082 =	9
10 =	2,20	10 =	6,21	4,535 =	10
15 =	3,30	15 =	9,32		
20 =	4,40	20 =	12,43		
30 =	6,60	30 =	18,64		
40 =	8,80	40 =	24,85		
50 =	11,00	50 =	31,07		
100 =	22,00	100 =	62,14		

Getting your boat back other ways

If your boat cannot make the 7 knots necessary to get back up the Rhône you may be interested to consider other ways; towing back up the Rhône has rather gone out of fashion since the river has been canalised, but facilities are still available.

Before deciding to go down the Rhône, of course, serious consideration should be given to the question of getting back up again but remarkably few cruising folk seem to consider this (and few need to consider it now with better performance craft widely in use. In fact it is commonplace to winter in the Mediterranean sun and come up the Rhône to explore new inland waterways in the spring and summer). Even in the days of the untamed Rhône, back in the days when we went through the Rove Tunnel to Marseille, we would be alongside in the Vieux Port and ask, 'How are you going to get back up again?', to be met with uncomprehending stares. Nobody was going back up again.

If you wished to return in your boat you had the alternative route via the Canal du Midi, Biscay, Villaine and Rance to St. Malo, assuming possession of the necessary sea-going experience for the open sea passages involved this way.

But those who allowed work to interfere with their yachting to the extent that they could only manage a limited time cruise rarely came down the Rhône.

Emergencies arise, however, recalling you from any part of France without your boat and it may then be of interest to know what facilities exist for bringing it back if you cannot do so.

Probably the first alternative that comes to mind is to employ a professional yacht 'deliverer'. There are quite a number and their advertisements can be seen in any of the yachting magazines. Any of them will be pleased to give you a quotation for bringing your boat back. Their charges vary somewhat but you can take it as a rough estimate that you would have to pay around £35 a day for a yacht that a two-man crew could handle. In addition you would have to pay fares out to the boat and all expenses of the boat on the journey home. Professional deliverers will usually quote either a lump sum figure or a rate per day; if they get back quickly (and they are highly efficient) you will regret having negotiated a lump sum arrangement. If they are held up by weather you will regret having negotiated a rate per day.

The next alternative is to seek an amateur crew who might like the chance of a trip for expenses only. The yachting magazines usually have a number of advertisements in their personal columns; you can also advertise yourself, of course. Some of the larger yacht

Miscellaneous

builders, like A. H. Moody and Camper and Nicholsons maintain registers of yachtsmen who are interested in crewing. If you decide to entrust the bringing back of your boat to an amateur yachtsman it is obviously up to you to satisfy yourself as to his competence to do so.

To bring a boat back by road costs around 40p a return mile plus the cost of the lift from and to the water. A number of firms advertise road transport of boats in the yachting magazines.

Another alternative is to consider bringing your boat back by easy stages, leaving her in the care of lock keepers where there is room to do so. At the majority of locks the waterway on either side would be impeded by a 'parked' yacht but there are sufficient with a little extra waterway space, or small harbour, where you see parked yachts of all nationalities. Many towns and villages have quays and harbours of varying sizes; in an increasing number of these there are now hire fleets moored. We have left boats here and there over the years and they have always been looked after.

If you are planning to be abroad for a long time it can be an expensive business fixing up Travel Insurance with an insurance company. Whether or not this is arranged, U.K. citizens should go to their local Department of Health and Social Security for a Form E111 which is a Certificate of Entitlement to Benefits in Kind during a stay in a Member State under the European Communities Social Security Regulations. I have reason to be grateful for this scheme since I was suddenly laid low when we were moored in the middle of Le Havre harbour. In no time at all a speedy craft was alongside with attendants in wet suits plus a charming lady doctor; an ambulance was waiting on the quay and I was being dealt with in a super-efficient hospital within the hour. Having been restored to health with great kindness and skill I can testify that the French medical authorities honour the reciprocal health agreement in splendid and charming fashion. I can only hope that we do as well for French nationals in need.

32.   Berry au Bac. Canal latéral à l'Aisne. Barge with wheelhouse folded down.

12 Route Details Section

LIMITS OF LENGTH AND BREADTH
(height above waterline and draft are shown above each route)

	Length m	Breadth m
RIVER SEINE—from Rouen to Corbeil	141,00	11,60
Canals linking Paris with Lyon via BURGUNDY	38,50	5,00
Canals linking Paris with Lyon via NEVERS and the BOURBONNAIS	38,50	5,00
Canals linking Paris with Lyon via the RIVER MARNE	38,50	5,00
Canals linking Paris with Northern France	38,50	5,00
Canals linking Paris with Belgium	38,50	5,00
Canals linking Paris with Strasbourg	38,50	5,00
Canal de la Marne à la Saône	38,50	5,00
Canal du Rhône au Rhin	33,70	5,10
Canal du Midi	30,00	5,25
Canal latéral à la Garonne	30,00	5,80
Nantes–Redon–Rennes–St. Malo	26,00	4,50

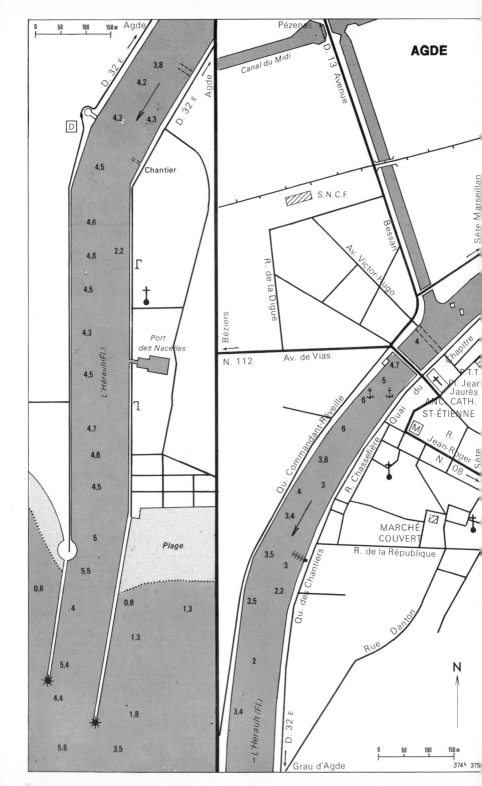

AGDE

Agde

0 50 100 150 m

D. 32 E

3,8

4,2

4,2   4,3

D
4,2

4,5   Chantier

4,6

4,8   2,2

4,5   ┌
       †

4,3

Port
des Nacelles

4,5

┐

4,7

4,6

4,5

L'Hérault (Fl.)

5

5,5

0,8
    4   0,6   1,3

      1,3

      Plage

5,4

4,4   1,8

5,6   3,5

Pézenas

Canal du Midi

D. 13 Avenue

Sète Marseillan

S.N.C.F.

Bessan

Av. Victor-Hugo

R. de la Digue

Béziers

N. 112   Av. de Vias

Qu. Commandant-Réveille

4

4,7

5
6 † ⚓

6

3,8

4   3

3,4

3,5

3   R. de la République

2,2

3,5

2

3,4

Qu. des Chantiers

Chapitre

P.T.T

Pl. Jean
Jaurès

ANC. CATH.
ST-ÉTIENNE

M   R.
Jean-Roger

N. 08

R. Chassefière

Qu. du

Sète

MARCHÉ
COUVERT

Rue Danton

D. 32 E

L'Hérault (Fl.)

Grau d'Agde

N

0 50 100 150 m

374b 375

Route 1 **Agde to Royan**

Distance	619km
Number of locks	131
Minimum height above water	3,47m
Minimum depth of water	1,45m

	Kms	Locks		Michelin Map No.
ETANG DU THAU			**SETE**	83
	19		**MARSEILLAN**	83
CANAL DU MIDI	3			
		3		
	8		**AGDE** (pop: 10 000). Old seaport and fishing port. 12thC church, was a cathedral. Museum, local folklore.	83
		5		
	24		**BEZIERS** (pop: 75 000). Centre of Hérault and Aude wine regions; in particular the town is associated with the red wine known locally as *Gros Rouge*. It is said that blancmange was invented here. Churches: St. Aphrodise, 11th–15thC; Madeleine, originally Romanesque. Museums: pictures, Greek vases, local interest and the wine trade. Garden of poets.	83
TUNNEL		9		
	13		**POILHES.** Nearby is Oppidum d'Ensérune, the only fully excavated pre-Roman city in France.	83
	6		**CAPESTANG**	83
(Left Canal to La Nouvelle) See Route 1A	21 13		**ROUBIA**	83
		8		
	13		**LA REDORTE**	83
		7		
	13		**MARSEILLETTE**	83
		1		
	10		**TREBES**	83
		6		
	11		**CARCASSONE** (pop: 40 000). Outstanding example of fortified medieval town with double	83

			Micheli
	Kms Locks	**Route 1**	*Map No*

CANAL DU MIDI   ramparts restored 19thC. Enclosed city fortress with 54 towers, but town has expanded beyond. Churches: St. Vincent, 14thC; St. Michael, 13thC. The wine-growing area of Corbières is situated in the foothills of the Pyrenees with Carcassone in the North West and the Mediterranean in the East. It is the largest producer of V.D.Q.S. wines in France and has one wine, Fitou, of *Appellation Contrôlée*. Strong red wines with pleasant bouquet are mainly produced.

	4		
13		**VILLESEQUELANDE**	8
	2		
11		**BRAM**	8
	11		
13		**CASTELNAUDARY** (pop: 10 000). Well known for *cassoulet*, a form of stew and for its cooking generally. 14thC church of St. Michel.	8
	5		
11		**SEGALA**	8
	6		
13		**GARDOUCH**	8
	4		
11		**MONTGISCARD**	8
	2		
21		**TOULOUSE** (pop: 325 000). Fourth largest city	8

33.   Carcassone.

34. Toulouse.

Photo Yan

	Kms	Locks	Route 1	Michelin Map N
CANAL DU MIDI			in France. Cultural and business centre. University established here over 700 years ago. Many old churches and fine houses. Museums: Delacroix, Corot, Ingrès, Poussin, Toulouse-Lautrec. Toulouse cathedral is said to be the most complete romanesque church in France.	
		6		
CANAL LATERAL	5			
A LA GARONNE		2		
	6		**FENOUILLET**	8
		4		
	10		**ST. JORY**	8
		3		
	11		**GRISOLLES**	8
	6		**DIEUPENTALE**	8
		1		
(Right Canal to Montauban)	16		**MONTAUBAN** (pop: 45 000). Capital of the department of Tarn-et-Garonne. Once a fortress. Famous bridge (the Tarn bridge). Church: St. Jacques, 14thC. Ingrès Museum: mainly pictures and drawing of Ingrès, also Delacroix, Poussin.	8
			MONTECH	82,7
		8		
	13		**CASTELSARRASIN**	7
		7		
	5		**MOISSAC** (pop: 10 000). Peaceful old town. Good market.	7
		4		
	16		**VALENCE D'AGEN**	7
		1		
	6		**LAMAGISTERE**	7
		2		
	19		**AGEN** (pop: 35 000). Capital of Lot-et-Garonne. Narrow streets in the old quarter giving way to broad boulevards. Fashionable shops. The name of Agen is associated with plums; try the plum preserve. St. Caprais Cathedral, 11th–16thC; Notre Dame, 13thC; St. Hillaire, 15thC. Museum: ceramics, furniture, tapestries, paintings, including Goya's self portrait; Gallo-Roman antiquities. Between Agen and Bayonne is the Region of Armagnac brandy. It is the oldest of French brandies prepared by slow continuous distillation from Gascon Picpoult grapes, Bas-Armagnac (black Armagnac) brandies are particularly sought after. The nearest distillery is at Condom, and	7

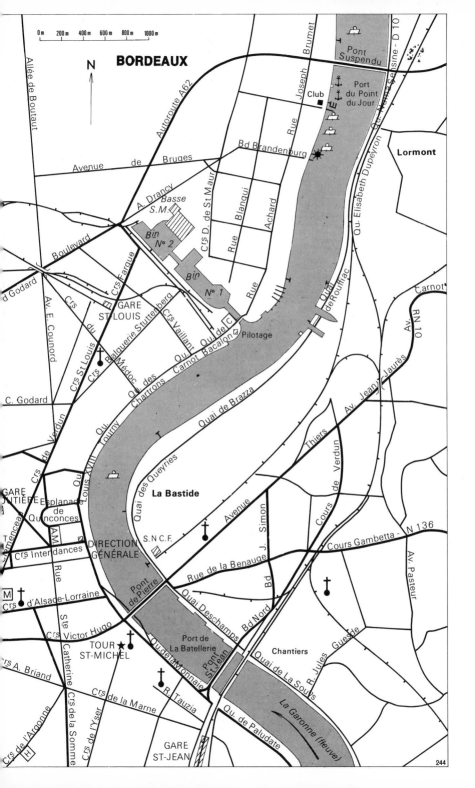

BORDEAUX

N

	Kms	Locks	Route 1	Michelin Map No.
CANAL LATERAL			visitors are welcome to look around.	
A LA GARONNE		7		
	27		**BUZET**	79
	3		**DAMAZAN**	79
		2		
	6		**TONNEINS**	79
		1		
	6		**LE MAS D'AGENAIS**	79
		4		
	18		**MEILHAN**	79
		6		
RIVER GARONNE	18		**CASTETS-EN-DORTHE**	79
	10		**LANGON.** A small area here produces Sauternes and Barsac, the best sweet wines in the world. Only white wines are produced here and they are naturally sweet. In this region the grapes are picked when they are over-ripe and each grape is picked individually. Thus each grape contains a large amount of sugar which gives the natural sweetness for which these wines are famous.	79,71
	6		**BARSAC**	79,71
	2		**CADILLAC**	79,71
	3		**PODENSAC**	79,71
	3		**PAILLET**	79,71
	2		**LESTIAC**	79,71
	11		**BAURECH**	79,71
	13		**BEGLES**	79,71
	5		**BORDEAUX** (pop: 250 000). Principal port, particularly for wine, and one of the most important industrial and tourist centres. Fifth largest city in France; centre of the most famous wine growing area in the world. Grand Théâtre, 1776–80. St. Andre Cathedral, 11thC; St. Seurin, 12th–15thC; Palais Gallien, 18thC. Remains of Roman amphitheatre. Museum: notable paintings, sculpture, and maritime. Real Bordeaux wine only comes from Bordeaux; the greater part of the annual Bordeaux crop is offered under district	71

names and wine from the best vineyards—less
than 10 per cent of the total—is usually sold under
the name of the château of origin. Bordeaux
Rouge, a rather light wine, covers all Bordeaux
wines not sold under another district name. Visits
to vineyards, cellars, also tasting can be arranged;
the *Syndicat d'Initiative* will provide latest
information. East of Bordeaux is St. Emilion, a
vineyard of repute in Roman times. The region of
St. Emilion produces not only St. Emilion itself,
but also wines whose names are made up of the
name St. Emilion preceded by the name of a
village. These wines are of a rich ruby colour.
Neighbouring districts include POMEROL,
COTES DE CANON FRONSAC, LALANDE
DE POMEROL, NEAC, COTES DE
FRONSAC, ST. GEORGES, LUSSAC,
MONTAGNE, PARSAC, and PUISSEGUIN.
Between the rivers Garonne and Dordogne is
produced the wine of Entre-Deux-Mers, a dry
white wine with a subtle bouquet. Above Bordeaux
the Médoc vineyards are planted on stony and

35. Bordeaux.

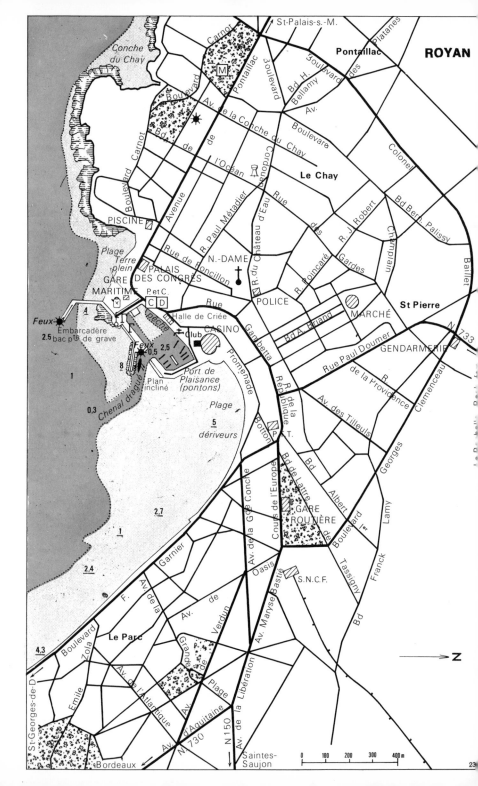

ROYAN

Conche
du Chay

St-Palais-s.-M.

Pontaillac

Platanes

M

Carnot

Pontaillac

Boulevard

Bd H.
Bellamy

Boulevard des

Av.

Boulevard

Colonel

Boulevard Carnot

Bd de

Av. de la Conche du Chay

Le Chay

de

l'Océan

R. du Château d'Eau

Rue

Champlain

Bd Berth. Palissy

Bailet

PISCINE

Avenue

de

R. Paul Métadier

des

R. J. Robert

St Pierre

N 733

Plage
Terre
plein

Rue de Foncillon

N.-DAME

R. Poincaré

Gardes

R.

MARCHÉ

La Rochelle Boston

GARE
MARITIME

PALAIS
DES CONGRES

P. et C.

C D

Rue

POLICE

Bd A. Briand

GENDARMERIE

Feux

4

Halle de Criée

Gambetta

CASINO

Rue Paul Doumer

Embarcadère
bac pte de grave

Club

de la Providence

R.

2.5

Feux
0,5

2.5

Port de
Plaisance
(pontons)

Promenade

Av. des Tilleuls

8

Plage

Clemenceau

Plan
incliné

5
dériveurs

Bd de la République

Bd de Lattre

Georges

1

0,3

Chenal dragué

Bd

Albert 1er

Lamy

2,7

Av. de la Gde Conche

P
T.

GARE
ROUTIÈRE

Boulevard

Tassigny

Franck

1

Garnier

Cours de l'Europe

S.N.C.F.

Bd

2,4

Av. de la

F.

Av.

de

Oasis

Av. Maryse Bastié

Le Parc

Boulevard

Verdun

Grande

Z

4,3

Emile

Zola

Av. de l'Atlantique

de

Plage

Av. de la Libération

St-Georges-de-D

Av. d'Aguitaine

N 150

Av. de

Saintes-
Saujon

N 730

Bordeaux

0   100   200   300   400 m

23

Kms Locks   **Route 1**

RIVER GARONNE   sandy ground on the left bank of the Gironde.
                                According to an old saying the vines must be
                                planted on stony ground and in sight of the river
                                for the wine to be good. Stretching from the Point
                                de Grave to Bordeaux the vineyard is divided into
                                two parts, Médoc in the North and Haut-Médoc
                                in the Southern part. Some of the finest red wines
                                in the world are produced here: Médoc is fine,
                                generally light red. The superior subdistricts
                                belonging to Haut-Médoc are ST. ESTEPHE,
                                PAUILLAC, ST. JULIEN, LISTRAC,
                                MOULIS, MARGAUX. To the right of the
                                Gironde are the seven districts where Cognac is
                                made. The town of Cognac is 6okm away.

(from Right River
Dordogne) From   21
this point the RIVER
GARONNE becomes the
RIVER GIRONDE 105   **ROYAN** (pop: 20 000). Popular seaside resort   71
                                with several beaches of fine sand. There are a
                                number of interesting examples of modern archi-
                                tecture, as a result of the destruction of the town
                                in World War II.

Route 1A **Branch from Canal du Midi to La Nouvelle**

Distance	37km
Number of locks	13
Minimum height above water	3,23m
Minimum depth of water	1,75m

	Kms	Locks		Michelin Map No
from CANAL DU MIDI			(near) **MIREPEISSET**	83
	3	5	**SALLELES**	83
		2		
RIVER AUDE	3			
CANAL DE LA ROBINE				
	8	3	**NARBONNE** (pop: 37 000). Interesting old	83,86

PORT-LA-NOUVELLE

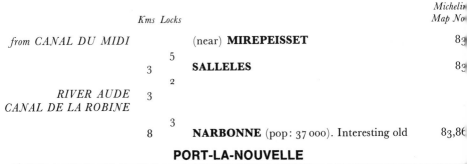

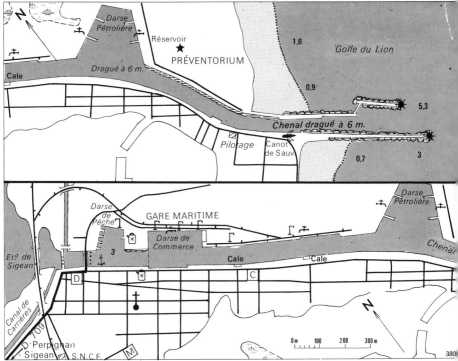

			Michelin
	Kms Locks	**Route 1A**	*Map No.*

CANAL DE LA ROBINE

town, a seaport long ago until silting up occurred. Boulevards now where ramparts used to be. 13thC former Archbishop's palace. Museum. The vineyards of Minervois, a wine-growing area since Roman times, are situated across the two departments of Aude and Hérault, beginning just above Carcassone and ending around Narbonne. The dry and warm climate produces a V.D.Q.S. wine of excellent quality, mostly red.

3

23   **PORT LA NOUVELLE** (pop: 2000). Small   86
commercial and fishing port with resort-type development. (See LANGUEDOC-ROUSSILLION in Route 2.)

The Canal du Rhône à Sète cannot now be reached through the lock opposite TARASCON as formerly. Entry to it is from the Rhône at K.279, into the Petit Rhône and through the Ecluse St. Giles at K.29.

Route 2 **Beaucaire to Sète**

Distance	103 km
Number of locks	2
Minimum height above water	4,75m
(but see Petit Rhône to	
Grau d'Orgon)	
Minimum depth of water	1,80m

Km Locks			*Michelin*
Mk			*Map No.*
0			**BEAUCAIRE** (pop: 11 000). Its fair, first held in 1217, was famous throughout Western Europe until the 19thC but is of little importance now. Wine shipping port. Ruins of 13thC castle; fine views over Rhône from remaining tower. Museum with local relics and items referring to the fair.
LOCK *DU NOURRIGUIER*	8	1	
JUNCTION with *PETIT RHONE*	29		

PETIT RHONE
to Grau d'Orgon

	Km Mk	Locks		Michelin Map No.
RIVER RHONE *turn RIGHT into* *PETIT RHONE* *(Km Mk numbering* *continues in* *sequence)*	279			
JUNCTION *str. on to GRAU* *D'ORGON, (maximum* *height 2,70m)*	299			
Care necessary *proceeding to sea.*	377		**GRAU D'ORGON**	

PETIT RHONE
to the Canal du Rhône à Sète

	Km Mk	Locks		
RIVER RHONE *turn RIGHT into* *PETIT RHONE* *(Km Mk numbering* *continues in* *sequence)*	279			
JUNCTION *turn RIGHT*	299			
LOCK *ST. GILLES*	300	I		
JOIN CANAL DU *RHONE A SETE.* *(Km Mk numbering of* *Canal du Rhône à Sète)*	29 50		**AIGUES-MORTES** (pop: 4000). Walled town with 17 towers and 10 gates, in the middle of swamps and lagoons from which its name (*aquae* *mortuae*, dead waters) derives. Founded by St. Louis in the 13thC as a Mediterranean seaport, but much silting up since. Church of St. Louis. 13th C. All facilities are available here, including fuel and water nearby.	83

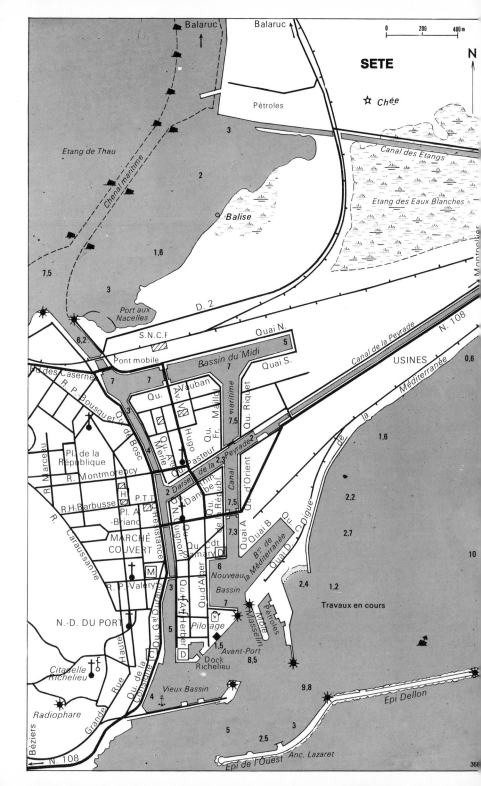

Km Mk	Locks	Route 2	Michelin Map No.
(Left Canal Maritime *to Le Grau du Roi*)* 75		**PALAVAS**	
92		**FRONTIGNAN**	
LEFT to SÈTE 96 *(Str. on to Bassin* *du Thau and across* *to Canal du Midi* *to join with* *Routes 1 and 1A)*		**SETE** (pop: 36 000). Interesting commercial port 83 with many canals lined with boats of all sorts. Busy fishing harbour and separate marina-type yacht harbour. Large export trade in wine.	

*Le Grau du Roi is part of the Languedoc-Roussillon development, the 190km of new holiday coast being constructed by the French Government, covering the area from the Rhône to the Spanish border. Tourists have always turned left as they approach Marseille, but the French Government now hope that they will be turning right in increasing numbers.

For nearly ten years, what was a barren coastline has been sprayed from helicopters in a massive anti-mosquito campaign, bulldozed and dredged on a massive scale.

As you cruise along the Beaucaire-Sète canal you can now see a hazy outline of houses, hotels, huge blocks of flats, the beginnings of what will be an endless frieze of concrete.

LE GRAU DU ROI has a planned capacity for 450 yachts with all facilities.

Next along the coast is LA GRANDE MOTTE, comprising the existing resorts of Palavas-les-Flots, Carnon-Plage and Le-Grau-du-Rois plus the new resort of La Grande Motte with a full capacity will be over 1000. Large scale development of flats, villas, shops and restaurants is well under way, with accommodation for 20 000 people in flats and hotels and 10 000 in villas. When building is finished here here will be room for 50 000.

L'EMBOUCHURE DE L'AUDE is sited at the mouth of the River Aude and embraces Valras Plage at the mouth of the Orb.

GRUISSAN takes in Saint-Pierre-sur-Mer, Narbonne-Plage, Gruissan village, and Gruissan Plage is planned to accommodate 50 000 with a harbour for 1500 boats.

LEUCATE-BARCARES is the largest of the six development schemes. Planned to accommodate 75 000 it will offer 20kms of canals and harbours for boats with 2000 moorings. Nearby Port La Nouvelle is the nearest exit to the Mediterranean from the Bordeaux end of the Canal du Midi, furthest if coming from the Rhône.

SAINT-CYPRIEN is planned to accommodate 24 000 and 1000 boats.

It is expected that the next few years will bring over 2 000 000 visitors to this new coast which is probably the biggest planned holiday development in the world.

Long marina-type piers stretch out in the new yacht harbours from the new concrete shore. Each of the thousands of moorings has its own electricity and water point laid on. The ultimate plan is to provide over 10 000 yacht berths at marinas spaced about 24kms apart. Although this is being developed in a holiday setting, the object is also to provide winter berthing at moderate charges.

Route 3 **Berry-au-Bac to Maxilly-a-Saone**

Distance		315km
Number of locks		147
Minimum height above water		3,50m
Minimum depth of water		2,13m

	Kms	Locks		Michelin Map No.
CANAL DE L'AISNE			**BERRY-AU-BAC**	56
A MARNE		6		
	10		**LOIVRE**	56
		3		
	13		**RHEIMS** (pop: 130 000). Splendid modern city, rebuilt after damage of two world wars. Many kings of France were crowned here. Centre of champagne producing region. Germans surrendered in Rheims in May 1945. Notre Dame cathedral, 13thC; St. Rémy church, 11thC. Museum: pictures (Delacroix, Latour, Bonnard, Gaugin, Matisse, Picasso, Pissarro, Renoir, Sisley), sculptures, tapestries. The following Champagne Cellars in Rheims can be visited: Veuve-Clicquot-Ponsardin, Pommery et Greno, Taittinger, Piper-Heidsieck, Mumm, Ruinart Pere et Fils, Abel Lepitre, Charles Heidsieck, George Goulet, Heidsieck & Co Monopole, Henriot, Lanson, Louis Roederer, and Masse Pere et Fils. Times	56
CANAL LATERAL A			and details from *Syndicat d'Initiative*. Most offer	
LA MARNE			free tasting.	
		4		
	11		**SILLERY**	56
		3		
	10		**SEPT-SAULX**	56
		2		
TUNNEL	3			
		8		
LEFT continuing CANAL	10		**CONDE-SUR-MARNE**	56
LATERAL A LA		2		
MARNE (Right to				
Epernay, River Marne)	16		**CHALONS-SUR-MARNE** (pop: 45 000). Capital of the department of Marne. Old town with a busy trade in wine, centre of the champagne country. Many fine buildings and pleasant tree-lined avenues. Suffered damage in both world	56

Kms	Locks	Route 3	Michelin Map No.

CANAL LATERAL A LA MARNE

wars. Variety of industry including Perrier. Cathedral, St. Etienne, 13thC. Churches: Notre-Dame en Vaux, 12thC; St. Loup, 15thC; St. Jean Baptiste, 11th–14thC. Museum: prehistoric, Gallo-Roman, Merovingian discoveries, sculptures, pictures.

Kms	Locks	Place	Map
11	3	**ST. GERMAIN-LA-VILLE**	56,61
10	1	**ABLANCOURT**	61
11	5	**VITRY-LE-FRANCOIS** (pop: 15 000). Once fortified town. Badly war damaged in 1940 and since rebuilt.	61
19	8	**PERTHES**	61
11	6	**ST. DIZIER** (pop: 35 000). Industrial town, rebuilt after disastrous 18thC fire. Part of old castle remains. St. Martin church, 13thC.	61,62
6	2	**CHAMOUILLEY**	61,62
10	5	**SOMMEVILLE**	61,62
13	6	**JOINVILLE.** Small old town. 16thC château.	61,62
13	6	**GUDMONT**	61,62
13	4	**VOUECOURT.** From here (or from Bologne eight kilometres further on) it is about 13 kilometres to COLOMBEY-LES-DEUX-EGLISES, where Général de Gaulle resided.	61,62
8	4	**BOLOGNE**	61,62
8	5	*TUNNEL*	
3	1	**CHAUMONT** (pop: 24 000). Pleasantly situated town. Fine buildings. Centre for manufacture of gloves and leather work. Headquarters of the American Army in World War I. Church: St. John, 13thC. Castle, 10thC.	61,62
13	8	**FOULAIN**	62
13	7	**ROLAMPOINT**	66
	5		

(Left Canal de la Marne au Rhin) STRAIGHT ON CANAL DE LA MARNE A LA SAONE

	Kms	Locks	Route 3	Michelin Map No.
	6		**HUMES**	66
CANAL DE LA MARNE A LA SAONE		3		
	5		**LANGRES** (pop: 8500). Old walled town in beautiful setting. St. Mammes Cathedral, 12thC. Two museums: sculptures, natural history, enamels, ivories, book-bindings.	66
		1		
	6		**BALESMES-SUR-MARNE**	66
TUNNEL				
	2		**HEUILLEY-COTTON**	66
		5		
	6		**VILLEGUSIEN**	66
		13		
	13		**CUSEY**	66
		13		
	23		**ATTRICOURT**	66
		5		
	8		**OISILLY**	66
		3		
	11		**MAXILLY-A-SAONE**	66

Route 4   **Berry-au-Bac to Troussey**

Distance	268km
Number of locks	86
Minimum height above water	3,35m
Minimum depth of water	1,98m

	Kms	Locks		Michelin Map No.
CANAL LATERAL A L'AISNE			**BERRY-AU-BAC**	56
		1		
	5		**VARISCOURT**	56
		1		
	2		**PIGNICOURT**	56
	2		**NEUFCHATEL-SUR-AISNE**	56
CANAL DES ARDENNES	5		**VIEUX-LES-ASFELD**	56
		2		
	5		**ASFELD**	56
		1		
	11		**TAIZY**	56
		1		
	5		**NANTEUIL-SUR-AISNE**	
	3		**RETHEL** (pop: 7000). Much damaged in both world wars and rebuilt twice. Church: St. Nicholas, 13thC. Folklore museum.	56
		3		
	11		**AMBLY**	56
		1		
	5		**GIVRY**	56
		1		
	3		**ATTIGNY**	56
		4		
	6		**SEMUY**	56
		7		
	3		**NEUVILLE**	56
		12		
	3		**MONTGON**	56
		4		
	3		**LE CHESNE**	56
		2		
	13		**AMBLY**	56

	Kms	Locks	Route 4	Michelin Map No
		1		
CANAL DES	3		**MALMY**	56
ARDENNES				
	3		**OMNICOURT**	53
TUNNEL				
		2		
	6		**HANNOGNE-ST.-MARTIN**	53
		2		
RIGHT into CANAL DE	2		**PONT-A-BAR**	53
L'EST (Left to River		1		
Meuse and Belgian frontier)	3		**DONCHERY**	53
		1		
	5		**GLAIRE**	53
		1		
	3		**SEDAN** (pop: 25 000). Busy industrial town. Much damaged in World War II, but now rebuilt.	53
		1		
	6		**REMILLY**	53,56
	3		**VILLERS-DEVANT-MOUZON**	53,56
		1		
	3		**MOUZON**	56
		2		
	10		**INOR**	56
		2		
	8		**STENAY**	56
		2		
	13		**DUN-SUR-MEUSE**	56
		3		
	10		**VILOSNES**	56
		2		
	8		**CONSEVOYE**	56
		1		
	2		**BRABANT-SUR-MEUSE**	5
		3		
	13		**BRAS-SUR-MEUSE**	5
	8		**VERDUN-SUR-MEUSE**	5
TUNNEL		3		
	6		**HAUDAINVILLE**	5
		2		
	8		**DIEUE**	5
	3		**GENICOURT-SUR-MEUSE**	5
	3		**AMBLY-SUR-MEUSE**	5
		2		
	5		**TROYON**	5

	Kms	Locks	Route 4	Michelin Map No.
		1		
CANAL DE L'EST	3		**LACROIX-SUR-MEUSE**	57
		1		
	5		**ROUVRAIS-SUR-MEUSE**	57
		1		
	6		**ST. MIHIEL**	57
		3		
	11		**SAMPIGNY**	57
		2		
	11		**COMMERCY** (pop: 8000). Pleasantly situated small town.	62
		1		
	8		**VERTUZEY**	62
(Right Canal de la Marne au Rhin)	5	4	**TROUSSEY**	62

Route 5 **Calais to Watten**

Distance	35km
Number of locks	1
Minimum height above water	3,55m
Minimum depth of water	2,28m

Kms Locks

Michel
Map N

CANAL DU CALAIS

CALAIS (pop: 75 000). Busy cross-channel port
and seaside resort with miles of fine sand. Much
damaged during World War II, rebuilt on modern
lines. English base during World War I. Nearest
French town to England. Calais and Dover were

5

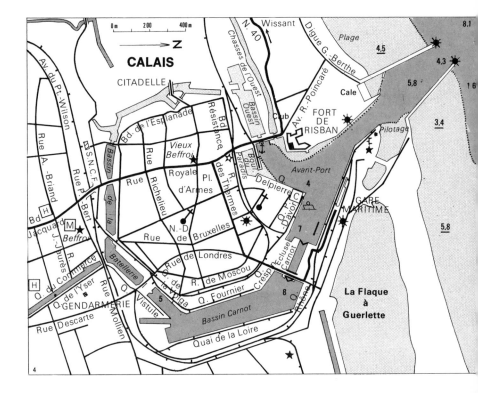

	Kms Locks	Route 5	*Michelin Map No.*

CANAL DU CALAIS first linked by a regular packet service over 200 years ago; Calais now receives 1 500 000 British travellers a year. Leading industry: machine lace and tulle. Museum: Flemish linen and lace, Rodin's 'Burghers of Calais'. War museum. Monuments.

(Right Canal de Guines)

(Right Canal d'Ardres) 11

(Right Canal d'Audruicq) 10

		1		
Turn RIGHT into RIVER AA	8		**PONT-DU-WEST**	51
	6		**WATTEN**	51

GRAVELINES et GRAND-FORT-PHILIPPE

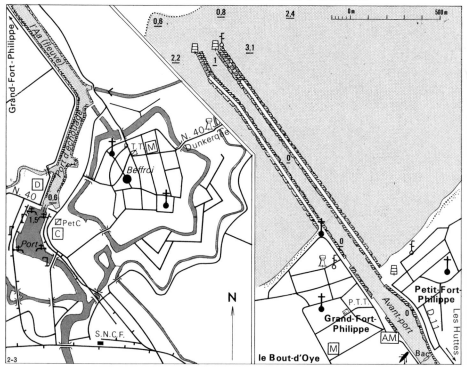

Route 5A **Gravelines to Watten**

Distance	18km
Number of locks	0
Minimum height above water	3,66m
Minimum depth of water	2,74m

Kms	Locks		Michelin Map No.
		FORT-PHILIPPE	51
RIVER AA			
		GRAVELINES (pop: 7000). Walled town.	51
	6		
eft Canal de Bourbourg)			
	6		
Right Canal du Calais)		**PONT-DU-WEST**	51
	6	**WATTEN**	51

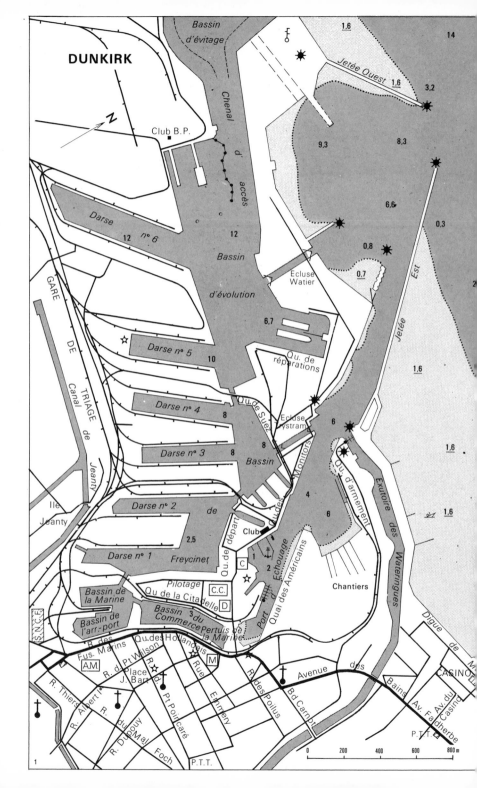

Route 5B **Dunkirk to Watten**

Distance	32km
Number of locks	3
Minimum height above water	3,66m
Minimum depth of water	2,13m

	Kms *Locks*		*Michelin* *Map No.*
ANAL DE BERGUES		**DUNKIRK** (pop: 28 000). Famous for the evacuation of the British Expeditionary Force in 1940 during which the town was almost completely destroyed; now rebuilt on modern lines. One of the most important seaports in France with big refineries and steelworks; connected to the inland industrial regions by four canals. Birthplace of Jean Bart, famous 17thC sailor.	51
rn RIGHT into CANAL LA HAUTE-COLME	8	**BERGUES** (pop: 5000). Small Flemish town with 17thC atmosphere, still surrounded by moats and ramparts. Much expert rebuilding following war damage. Museums: Brueghel, Jordaens, Van Dyck, Rubens. Natural history.	51
(Left Canal de la Basse-Colme)	3		
	24	**WATTEN**	51

Route 6 **Châlon-sur-Saône to Lyon**

Distance	140km
Number of locks	5
Minimum height above water	3,45m
Minimum depth of water	1,98m

	Kms	*Locks*		*Michelin Map No*
RIVER SAONE			**CHALON-SUR-SAONE**	7⊂
		1		
	31		**TOURNUS** (pop: 7000).	7⊂
	10		**UCHIZY.** Nearby wine village of Chardonnay.	7⊂
	5		**PORT FLEURVILLE**	7⊂
	19		**MACON** (pop: 26 000). Busy commercial town in the centre of wine-growing country, the Mâconnais. Old walled gardens and vineyards. Birthplace of Lamartine. Cathedral remains, 13thC, used as archaeological museum. The Mâconnais white grapes (Pinot, Chardonnay) give Mâcon Blanc and the Pouillys (especially Pouilly-Fuisse) the characteristic nutty flavour. The black Gamay grape produces the sprightly Mâcon Rouge and Mâcon Rosé. Nearby wine villages of Solutré, Pouilly, Fousse. Along the Saône are the BEAUJOLAIS villages, producing a soft, fruity wine, best drunk young and fresh. On the granite slopes West and Northwards are the great vineyards of St. Amour, Julienas, Chenas, Moulin-à-Vent, Fleurie, Chiroubles, Morgon, and Brouilly, delicate, light, lively wines with a rich bouquet.	7⊂
	6		**CRECHES.** Nearby wine villages of St. Amour (tasting at Caveau St. Amour), Julienas.	7⌐
	6		**ST. ROMAN-DES-ILES.** Nearby wine villages of Chenas, le Moulin-à-Vent (tasting at Caveau au Pied du Moulin), Fleurie.	7⌐
	3		**THOISSEY** (pop: 1000). Nearby wine villages of Chiroubles, Morgon.	7⌐
		1		

	Kms	*Locks*	**Route 6**	*Michelin Map No.*
RIVER SAONE	10		**BELLEVILLE-SUR-SAONE.** Nearby wine village of Brouilly.	73
	3		**MONTMERLE-SUR-SAONE**	73
	11		**VILLEFRANCHE-SUR-SAONE** (pop: 25 000). Important industrial town and wine centre. Interesting old houses. Notre-Dame church, 12thC.	73
	10	1	**TREVOUX**	73
	10	2	**NEUVILLE-SUR-SAONE**	73
	16		**LYON** (pop: 550 000). Third largest city in France. Centre of textile industry, particularly silk weaving, but much other industry besides. The most important buildings and shops are in the area between the Rhône and the Saône and adjacent to the yacht mooring. The hill of Fourvière with the modern church of Notre-Dame at its summit may be ascended by funicular railway. Churches: St. Martin, 11thC; St. Nizier, 15thC. Museum: old furniture, tapestries, water colours, coins. Collection of Oriental carpets. Also Delacroix, Gaugin, Manet, Renoir.	73

36. Lyon.

Route 7 **Chauny to Berry-au-Bac**

Distance	67km
Number of locks	13
Minimum height above water	3,37m
Minimum depth of water	2,21m

	Kms	Locks		Michelin Map No.
CANAL LATERAL A L'OISE				
			CHAUNY	56
LEFT into CANAL DE L'OISE A L'AISNE (Right to Compiègne)	2			
		1		
	2		**BICHANCOURT**	56
	5		**CHAMPS**	56
	3		**GUNY**	56
		3		
	11		**ANIZY**	56
		3		
	11		**PARGNY-FILAIN**	56
TUNNEL				
		1		
	6		**BRAYE-EN-LAONNOIS**	56
		4		
	6		**BOURG-ET-COMIN**	56
LEFT into CANAL LATERAL A L'AISNE (Right to Soissons)	5		**MAIZY**	56
		1		
	16		**BERRY-AU-BAC**	56

Route 8 Chauny to Conflans St. Honorine

Distance	133km
Number of locks	11
Minimum height above water	4,04m
Minimum depth of water	2,44m

	Kms	Locks		Michelin Map No.
ANAL LATERAL A L'OISE (Left Canal de l'Oise à l'Aisne)	2		**CHAUNY**	56
	3		**ABBECOURT**	56
	5		**APPILLY**	56
	16	2	**PIMPREZ**	56
	2		**RIBECOURT**	56
	3	1	**MONTMACQ**	56
	3	1	**LONGUEIL**	56
RIVER OISE	2		**JANVILLE**	56
(Left River Aisne)	3			
	2		**COMPIEGNE** (pop: 38 000).	56

COMPIEGNE (pop: 38 000). A popular place for tourists attracted by the great palace and enormous forest (33 000 acres, one of the largest in France), for long a favourite hunting resort of the kings of France. Joan of Arc was captured here on 23 May 1430 by John of Luxembourg who handed her over to the English. The palace is now a museum; the rooms occupied by Marie Antoinette, Napoléon I and III can be seen; also the National Automobile Museum with 150 vehicles ranging from the Roman chariot to the Citroën chain-track car. Nearby in the forest is the clearing in which Marshal Foch received the German surrender in November 1918; and where Hitler received the French surrender in 1940. The original railway saloon car was destroyed in World War II, but a replica may be seen. Town Hall

	Kms	Locks	Route 8	Michelir Map No
RIVER OISE			Museum: historical miniature figures, the only French museum of lead soldiers (90 000), with a large scene of the Battle of Waterloo.	
		I		
	6		**JAUX**	56
		I		
	10		**VERBERIE**	56
		I		
	11		**PONT ST. MAXENCE**	56
	8		**VILLERS ST. PAUL**	56
	3		**CREIL** (pop: 20 000). Industrial town. Church: St. Médard, 12thC.	56
		I		
	3		**ST. LEU-D'ESSERENT**	56
	6		**PRECY-SUR-OISE**	56
	3		**BORAN-SUR-OISE**	56
		I		
	10		**BEAUMONT-SUR-OISE**	55
	3		**CHAMPAGNE-SUR-OISE**	55
		I		
	3		**L'ISLE-ADAM**	55
	13		**PONTOISE** (pop: 19 000). Interesting old town with hilly, narrow streets. Churches: St. Maclou, 12thC; Notre-Dame, 13thC.	55
		I		
	13		**CONFLANS ST. HONORINE**	55

Route 9 **Compiègne to Bourg-et-Comin**

Distance 65km
Number of locks 10
Minimum height above water 3,35m
Minimum depth of water 2,05m

	Kms	Locks		Michelin Map No.
RIVER OISE			**COMPIEGNE**	56
Turn RIGHT into RIVER AISNE		3		
	18		**ATTICHY**	56
	6	1	**VIC-SUR-AISNE**	56
	18	2	**SOISSONS** (pop: 32 000). Industrial town, much damaged in both world wars and since rebuilt. Cathedral: St. Gervais, 12thC.	56
	11	1	**MISSY**	56
	5		**CONDE-SUR-AISNE**	56
GHT to CANALIZED SECTION	5	2	**CYS-LA-COMMUNE**	56
	2	1	**BOURG-ET-COMIN**	56

37. Briare. Canal latéral à la Loire. Pont canal, 640m long, built by Eiffel in 18 carry the Briare Canal over the River Loire.

Route 10 **Laroche to Decize**

Distance	188km
Number of locks	117
Minimum height above water	2,67m
Minimum depth of water	1,57m

	Kms	Locks		Michelin Map No.
RIVER YONNE (Left Canal de Bourgogne)		2	**LAROCHE**	65
	6	7	**BASSOU**	65
	16		**AUXERRE** (pop: 34 000). Capital of the department of Yonne. Centre of wine and beautiful district of vineyards and orchards. An old town built on a hill, a most attractive sight from the river. St. Germain's Abbey, Caroligian crypts, 9thC frescoes (the oldest mural paintings in France), 12thC Romanesque spire. St. Etienne, 13thC. Museums with Napoleonic souvenirs, early French paintings, tapestries.	65
CANAL DU NIVERNAIS		9		
	13	9	**VINCELLES**	65

38. Auxerre.

	Kms	Locks	Route 10	Michelin Map No.
CANAL DU NIVERNAIS	18		**MAILLY-LE-CHATEAU**	65
		9		
	19		**COULANGES-SUR-YONNE**	65
		6		
	10		**CLAMECY** (pop: 6000). The old city of the Counts of Nevers, situated at the confluence of the Yonne and the Beuvron, a cultural centre, the birthplace of Romain Rolland and Claude Tillier.	65
		6		
	10		**BREVES**	65
		5		
	11		**DIROL**	65
		8		
	10		**CHAUMOT**	65
		10		
	6		**SARDY-LES-EPIRY**	65
		15		
	3		**LA COLLANCELLE**	65
TUNNEL				
		7		
	13		**MONT-ET-MARRE**	69
		4		
	6		**CHATILLON-EN-BAZOIS**	69
		6		
	13		**FLEURY**	69
		4		
	8		**PANNECOT**	69
		5		
	13		**CERCY-LA-TOUR**	69
		5		
	13		**DECIZE** (pop: 7500). An old town with a church built on a 7thC crypt. Promenade des Halles leads to the beach and water sports stadium.	69

Route 11 **Le Havre to Paris**

Distance	364km
Number of locks	7
Minimum height above water	5,97m
Minimum depth of water	3,18m

Because LE HAVRE is the most popular entry port into France, the alternatives here
ll be dealt with at some length.

On arrival at Le Havre a yacht should turn hard to port immediately on passing through
 harbour entrance and proceed to the appropriate yacht moorings ahead in the Ports des
chts (extended since drawing of map on page 134).

Sailing yachts can have their masts unstepped here by a small crane on the jetty for a
rge of around 11 francs.

From Le Havre it is possible in a yacht of only moderate speed to reach Rouen (128km)
one tide going straight up the Seine. From the Petit Port, returning out of the harbour
ance and across to the entrance of the Seine will take approximately an hour. It is
isable to have Admiralty Chart 2990. Obviously it is essential to be ready moving up the
e just before the first of the flood. In good weather this is the easiest, quickest, and most
eable way of reaching Rouen.

An alternative to LE HAVRE, about 20kms away up the Seine, is HONFLEUR, but it is

39.   Petit Port, Le Havre.

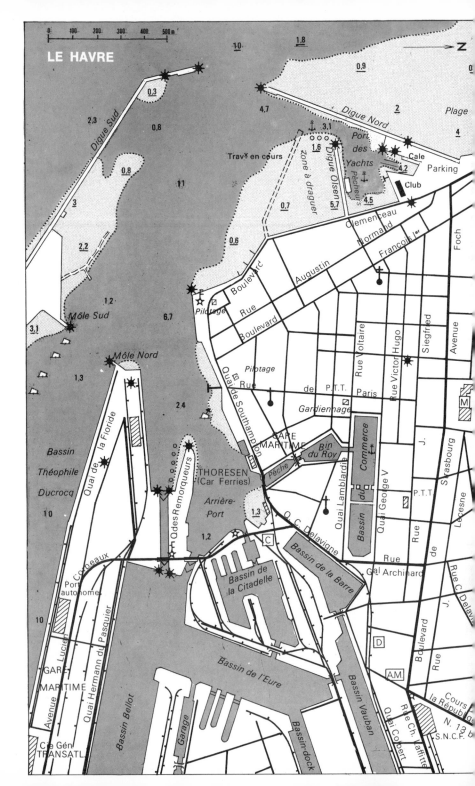

ecessary to lock in and out here with the inevitable wait for the tide. The locks open for
bout an hour either side of high water.)

On several tides each side of springs and particularly at equinoctial springs, the tidal bore
henomenon known as the Mascaret occurs in the lower Seine almost to Rouen. Reaching its
reatest magnitude at Caudebec, a wave height of 6m can occur there if there is a westerly
ind. Victor Hugo lost his eldest daughter and her husband in the Mascaret of 4 September
843; they were drowned in front of his house at Villequier. Since then the power of the
Iascaret has been much lessened by various river works, but it is still a consideration to be
ken into account when planning the time-table of a voyage up the Seine.

Having reached the Petit Port, if the weather outside is bad it is not necessary to leave the
rotection of Le Havre harbour. An alternative route is to proceed through Le Havre docks
nd up the Tancarville Canal (24km, 2 locks), a slower and less pleasant waterway.

To reach the Tancarville Canal from the Petit Port the correct route is via the Avant
ort, Arrière Port, Bassin de la Citadelle, Bassin de l'Eure, Bassin Fluvial (*not* the Bassin Bellot
hich is for big ships only), Bassin Vétillart, and so to the Canal de Tancarville.

On arrival at Tancarville Lock it will almost certainly be necessary to wait for locking in.
ecure out of the way of commercial traffic, between the mooring posts and the bank, for
stance, rather than on the 'channel' side of the posts.

The Tancarville Lock opening schedule is linked to the times of the Seine tides; you will
nly be let out into the Seine at the right time.

On coming out of the Tancarville Lock a good look-out must be kept for traffic coming
own the Seine as it will obviously be necessary to cross the path of this traffic to get to the
orrect side of the river.

Craft with sufficient power usually proceed straight up the Seine to Rouen without
opping at Le Havre.

40.   Bassin du Commerce, Le Havre.

Kms	Locks	Route 11	Michelin Map No.

RIVER SEINE

LE HAVRE (pop: 200 000). The second largest seaport in France and principal transatlantic port in the country. It suffered greater damage in World War II than any other port. Rebuilding of the town was carefully planned with wide streets; the first of these seen on coming from the yacht harbour at the Petit Port is the Avenue Foch leading to the Town Hall Square.   55

HONFLEUR (pop: 9000). Picturesque houses round the old harbour are an attractive feature of this charming old town. The church of St. Catherine was built of wood by local shipbuilders. Fishing boats and yachts use the harbour; despite need to lock in and out, many yachtsmen prefer it to Le Havre.   55

21   **TANCARVILLE.** Tancarville Bridge, the longest suspension bridge in Europe, was completed in 1959.

33   **CAUDEBEC-EN-CAUX.** Picturesque little timber-built town, largely destroyed in World War II. Popular place to view the Mascaret.   55

13   **JUMIEGES.** Ruins of ancient abbey founded 654.   55

58   **ROUEN** (pop: 370 000). Important industrial town (textiles); although inland is the third seaport   55

41.   Rouen.   *Photo R. Manson*

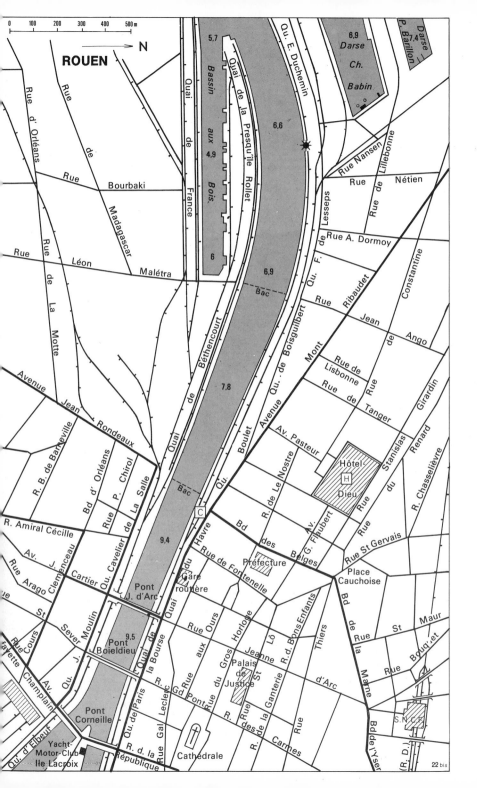

ROUEN

N

0 100 200 300 400 500 m

Qu. E. Duchemin

6,9
Darse
Ch.
Babin

7,4
Darse
P. Barillon

5,7

4,9

6

Bassin aux Bois

Quai de France

Quai de la Presqu'île Rollet

6,6

6,9

Bac

7,8

Béthencourt

Quai de

9,4

Bac

C

9,5

Havre

Rue de Fontenelle

Gare routière

Pont J. d'Arc

Pont Boieldieu

Quai de la Bourse

Quai de Paris

R. Gal Leclerc

Gd Pont

Pont Corneille

Yacht-Motor-Club Île Lacroix

Qu. d'Elbeuf

R. d. la République

Cathédrale

Palais de Justice

Rue aux Ours

Rue de l'Horloge

Rue du Gros

Rue Jeanne

St Lô

R. d. Bons Enfants

Rue de la Ganterie

Rue des Carmes

Rue d'Arc

Rue St Gervais

Place Cauchoise

Bd de Rue

Thiers

St Maur

Rue Bouquet

Rue de la Marne

Bd de l'Yser

(R. D.)

S.N.C.F.

Rue Nansen

Rue Netien

Rue de Lillebonne

Rue de Nétien

Lesseps

de

Rue A. Dormoy

Qu. F. de

Qu. de Boisguilbert

Rue Ribaudet

Rue Jean

de

Ango

Mont

Rue de Lisbonne

Rue de Tanger

Stanislas

Rue du

Renard

R. Chasselièvre

Girardin

Constantine

Av. Pasteur

Hôtel-Dieu
H

Av. G. Flaubert

Bd des Belges

R. de Le Nostre

Préfecture

Avenue Boulet

Qu.

Bd

Rue d'Orléans

Rue de

Bourbaki

Rue Madagascar

Rue Léon

Malétra

Rue de La Motte

Avenue Jean Rondeaux

R. B. de Barneville

Bd d' Orléans

Rue P. Chirol

Qu. Cavelier de La Salle

R. Amiral Cécille

Av. J. Clémenceau

Cartier

Rue Arago

St Sever

J. Moulin

Av. J.

Cours Champlain

La Fayette

22 bis

RIVER SEINE

in France with 24km of docks and wharves. Much damaged in World War II and rebuilt on modern lines. Joan of Arc was burned alive in Rouen in 1431; the site on the Place du Vieux-Marche is marked and there is a statue nearby of Joan at the stake. Cathedral: Notre-Dame, 13thC. Museum: fine arts, one of the best in France, Corot, Delacroix, Fragonard, Ingrès, Monet, Renoir, Sisley. Bassin St. Gervais is the usual berth if stopping for the night, but it is not very near to the town. A sailing yacht cannot proceed beyond Rouen without unstepping the mast.

24   **ELBEUF** (pop: 19 000). Industrial town, centre   55
of cloth making industry.

      1

35   **MUIDS**   55

10   **LES ANDELYS** (pop: 6000). Pretty little place   55
in beautiful situation, by the Forest of Andelys. Château Gaillard ruins, built by Richard the Lionheart in 1196.

      1

24   **VERNON** (pop: 16 000). Pleasant town. Notre-   56
Dame Church, 12thC. Tour Guise erected by

42.   Château Gaillard, Les Andelys.

Kms	Locks	Route 11	Michelin Map No.
RIVER SEINE		King Henry I of England.	
	1		
10		**BONNIERES**	55
	1		
21		**MANTES** (pop: 15 000). Old town in pretty situation. Much damaged in World War II but 12thC Notre-Dame church survived. William the Conqueror fatally injured here in falling from his horse.	55
	1		
18		**MEULAN** (pop: 5000). Old town.	55
(Left River Oise)	1		
24		**CONFLANS ST. HONORINE.** Home base of the barge trade. Note the barge painted white and bearing a cross; this is the floating chapel of the *bateliers*.	55
	1		
23		**BOUGIVAL**	55
50		**PARIS** (pop: 3 000 000). The Touring Club de France 3-deck Headquarters boat is on the port side immediately past Pont Alexandre III but their moorings extend from Pont Invalides to Pont de la Concorde. There are other moorings in Paris, but this is most central, provides the best facilities	55

43. Touring Club de France, Paris.

	Kms	Locks	Route 11	Michelin Map No.

RIVER SEINE

and information. A few steps from the T.C.F. mooring is the Place de la Concorde and the Tuileries Gardens. Also on the same side of the river, The Louvre, Palais Royal, Comédie Française, Avenue de l'Opéra, Opéra House, the Grand Boulevards, Madeleine Church, rue Royale, rue de la Paix, Place Vendôme, rue de Rivoli, Faubourg Saint-Honoré, Avenue des Champs-Elysées connecting the Place de la Concorde with the Place de l'Etoile, and the Arc de Triomphe.

On the other side of the river, The Palais Bourbon (National Assembly), Quai d'Orsay (Foreign Office), Esplanade des Invalides, the Hôtel des Invalides with the tombs of Napoléon and Marshal Foch, the Eiffel Tower. Worth a visit is the Musée des Caves de la Tour Eiffel, under the Chaillot Hill, Square Charles Dickens,

44.   A great deal of river traffic passes.

Kms Locks **Route 11**

RIVER SEINE

Paris 16; with mile-long galleries, wine museum, history of wine, a guided tour, and wine tasting.

The Touring Club Headquarters offers hot showers, bar and restaurant facilities, fuel and water. They are very helpful with any tourist query, but particularly with up-to-date news of the state of the waterways. English speaking staff are available much of the time.

However, during the day there is a great deal of river traffic past the T.C.F. moorings—barge, Coche d'Eau, Bateau Mouche, and Vedette Tour Eiffel—setting up a continuous swell. This is no inconvenience if you leave your craft for sightseeing during the day and only return at night when all is quiet; but the movement is so severe at times that no movable object on board should be left unsecured.

The whole magic of Paris is a warp's length

45. Bateau Mouche.

Photo Lucien Viguier

Kms Locks   **Route 11**

RIVER SEINE   away from the T.C.F. moorings; whilst marvelling
at this, skippers may spare a thought for their
female crew scrambling up the quay wall in jeans
and anorak to mix with the impeccable style of
Parisian shops and women.

46.   A scramble up the quay wall.

Route 12 **Lyon to Arles**

Distance	283km
Number of locks	11
Minimum height above water	
(canalized)	about 7m
	each bridge shows height on marker
	displayed before it
(uncanalized)	5,95m
Minimum depth of water	
(canalized)	3,20m
(uncanalized)	can be as low as 1,40m in autumn
	but see note re Chasse Gauge

t takes about two days to go down the Rhône from Lyon to Arles. As already described,
st of it is now canalized, straight lines of man-made banks and man-made water levels as
rly defined and smooth as the water in your bath, much more confidence inspiring than the
irregular banks of scrub and bush and trees (many drawn into the stream), and rock and
swirling, raging current.

oon after you leave Lyon and pass through the Pierre-Bènite lock you come to the
analized section, (at the time of writing the Ecluse de Vaugris was still under construction,
last lock and section to be completed). Since this is at Km. Mark 33 and the Km. Mark
nbering starts from the Lyon end you will see that you soon put the uncanalized section of
Rhône behind you.

ncidentally, you will note that because of the new derivations the Km. marks do not
ays follow a sequence nor tally up with the old Km. marks.

lthough placid looking and calm and tamed you will find that the canalized Rhône still runs
ngly and that this varies somewhat according to the width of the canal.

he Rhône locks, (195m long and 12m wide), are awe inspiring, deep as a cathedral, yet need
se no concern in passing for the water level changes—with you sitting upon it—without so
ch as a ripple. All Rhône locks are controlled by traffic lights; buzzers aquaint you with the
operation, that is the raising and lowering of the safety barriers in the front of the upper
es and the opening and closing of the gates/shutters and the movement of the water. Floating
lards, set in the lock walls, carry your warps up or down with you so that no adjustment is
essary.

Vhen going down proceed with care out and under the lifting gates/shutters and look out for
siderable quantities of debris collected there.

t some of the locks you may be asked for details of boat and owner, (Green Card or
tificate of Registry).

oing down, with the stream, the markers are red and white to starboard and black to port,
ept from K.146 to K.150 where green and white markers take the place of black). It is
ommended that you keep 20m away from the marks; at K.89 you keep 100m from the left
k to pass the King's Table.

he depth of water in the uncanalized section is not a problem except from August to
ober. If in doubt, before setting off to the Pierre-Bènite lock, you can telephone Lyon
73 05 15 to receive an automatic recording of the Chasse Gauge, a formula of the depth
ilable; but you must allow at least 1m on top of this.

It is not likely that you will have reason to go on deck but if you do you should wear a life-jacket; having an anchor ready is another precaution that should be observed.

If you propose 'turning left' when you reach the Mediterranean you will approach it from the Rhône through Port Louis, the Arles-Fos Canal being much too industrialized. If you propose 'turning right' when you reach the Mediterranean you will turn in to the Petit Rhône just before Arles and by Km. Mark 279, proceeding either to the sea at Grau d'Orgon or through the lock at St. Gilles to join the Canal du Rhône à Sète.

I would like to reiterate that fuelling alongside facilities are few and far between. Jerry cans are essential and topping up of fuel and water should be carried out whenever opportunity offers.

One can only stop at certain places and you MUST find a place early; you cannot go down the Rhône at night. (Locks open from 0500 to 2100 hours.)

47. Arles.

	Km Mk	Locks	Route 12	Michelin Map No.

RIVER SAONE   **LYON**   73

RRE-BENITE LOCK   4   I

RIVER RHONE   29   **VIENNE** (pop: 28 000). Ancient town important   73
in Roman times, but also developed industrially,
en K.17 and K.39 is the particularly textiles. Roman Temple of Augustus
t remaining section of the and Livia, 25 B.C. Roman Theatre and many
Rhône to be canalized— other Roman remains. The Côtes-du-Rhône
1978–1980) vineyards stretch right along the River Rhône.
There are two wine-growing regions, and these are
separated from each other by a zone of approximately 64km where there are no vineyards. In the
northern region, which stretches from Vienne
down to Valence, the land rises steeply from the
river valley and the vines grow on the terraced
hillsides. Almost opposite Vienne, on the other
bank of the river, one of the most famous and
oldest of all the Côtes-du-Rhône red wines is
produced, the Côte Rôtie, which has been
appreciated since Roman times for its richness.

LOCK DE VAUGRIS   34   I
(in construction)

41   **CONDRIEU.** Here is produced the distinctive   73
Condrieu, also the rare Château Grillet. For wine-
tasting, enquiries should be made at the Pavilion
de Tourisme. Not a very good mooring here at
the moment.

LOCK DE PEAGE   61   I
LOCK ST. VALLIER-
DE-GERVANS   86   I

91   **TOURNON** (pop: 6500). Busy old town. Near   77
here, on the West bank, are produced the full-
flavoured red and white St. Joseph wines, the red
Cornas, and the sparkling white St. Peray. On the
opposite bank are the districts of Crozes Hermitage,
producing the full-bodied red and delicate white
Hermitage wines. There is a small harbour
here, through which the current runs strongly; the
jetty is at rather an awkward height. Good shops.

LOCK BOURG-LES-   105   I
VALENCE
108   **VALENCE** (pop: 55 000). Prosperous old town   77
with many interesting historical associations.
11thC Cathedral. You can moor by the bridge
but there is also a fine marina at K.112.

	Km Mk	Locks	Route 12	Michelin Map No

LOCK BEAUCHASTEL 124 1

133   **LE POUZIN.** Not a very good mooring.   8

LOCK DE BAIX-LOGIS-NEUF 142 1

148   **RELAIS DE ROCHES.** A helpful little   7
LOCK CHATEAUNEUF-DU-RHONE 164 1   harbour with all the services your boat needs.   8

166   **VIVIERS** A fascinating old town; just up the old Rhône. A rather rough quay and a tiny, unsuitable harbour.

LOCK BOLLENE, DE ST. PIERRE 187 1   **BOLLENE** (pop: 9000). An old town, once   8 owned by the monks of Avignon, with remains of 14thC defences. Tree-lined promenades and some fine houses indicate former splendour. Many new industries are flourishing now. Bollène lies on the Donzère-Mondragon Canal, built in 1948–52 as part of a plan to regulate the Rhône and utilize it as a source of hydro-electric power. The André Blondel Usine-Barrage is the largest in Western Europe. From Bollène extends the southern region of the Côtes-du-Rhône; the vineyards are located east of Orange and on both sides of the Rhône.

LOCK DE CADEROUSSE 216 1

224   **ROQUEMAURE.** Opposite is CHATEAUNEUF-   8 DU-PAPE where the noted wines of that name are produced; heir to the wines used by the Popes for Mass (14thC). Beyond Roquemaure are the villages of TAVEL and LIRAC.

LOCK D'AVIGNON 234 1

244   turn back up to
AVIGNON (pop: 75 000). Great art town, most   80,83 interesting and well known as the temporary residence of the Popes. The Palace of the Popes was built 1335–67, on a hill overlooking the town and the Pont d'Avignon of nursery rhyme fame. Museums: antiques, pictures. Across the river is Villeneuve-lès-Avignon, summer residence of Popes. Good mooring but rather a noisy berth on the quay.

| | | Michelin
Map No. |

| Km
Mk | Locks | **Route 12** | Michelin
Map No. |

247   turn back up to
Port de Plaisance at
LA COURTINE. There are quayside fuel
pumps here. If you draw more than 1,60m look
out for the bar at the entrance to the Durance.

OCK DE TARASCON 265   1   **TARASCON** (Pop: 8500). Attractive old
town, opposite Beaucaire. Castle of Tarascon,
14thC, Prominent. No moorings here.

'URN to STARBOARD
n the PETIT RHONE
'ROCEEDING WEST
(See Route 2)

279
283   **ARLES** (pop: 42 000). An ancient town, a capital   83
city in Roman times with many important Roman
and medieval buildings. Roman theatre, amphitheatre, alyscamps, necropolis. The forum, on the
site of the Roman forum, is still the town centre.
Two stories of the amphitheatre, with sixty arches
each, are fairly well preserved. Roman theatre built
in the time of Augustus, but little remains. The
church, once cathedral, of St. Trophime is
supposed to have been founded in 606. With the
most southerly bridge over the Rhône forming a
link between Italy and Spain, Arles is situated
where the Rhône divides into two channels to form
the Camargue. Three museums: Roman and
pagan art; also Picasso, Matisse, Gaugin, Utrillo.
Bull fights. Mooring in the Rhône here is
difficult and most uncomfortable. The best
place to secure is in the basin through the new
lock; to reach it proceed down the Rhône for
almost a kilometre and turn back up, through
the lock, to Arles. There is a boatyard here.

Route 12A **Arles to Fos-sur-Mer**

Distance	47km
Number of locks	4
Minimum height above water	3,7m
Minimum depth of water	2m

	Kms	Locks		Michelin Map No.
CANAL D'ARLES A FOS			**ARLES**	83
		4		
	37		**FOS-SUR-MER**	84

Less than a kilometre from the second Arles bridge you turn in through 140° to port to the new lock. The whole area is dominated by belching chimneys, factories and refineries and it is certainly a most unattractive front door to the Mediterranean. Developed as a major tanker port it is not intended to appeal to the cruising yachtsman of course.

Route 12B **Arles to Port St. Louis**

Distance	39km
Number of locks	1
Minimum height above water	0
Minimum depth of water	1,45m

	Kms	Locks		Michelin Map No.
RIVER RHONE	284		**ARLES**	83
TURN back up LEFT *rough 140° to enter into* *ST. LOUIS CANAL*	323	1	**PORT ST. LOUIS.** Small port surrounded by the sights, sounds, and smells of heavy industry. Tie up at the boatyard where the service is most helpful. There is a crane available for stepping masts, also water on the quay.	84

PORT-SAINT-LOUIS-DU-RHONE

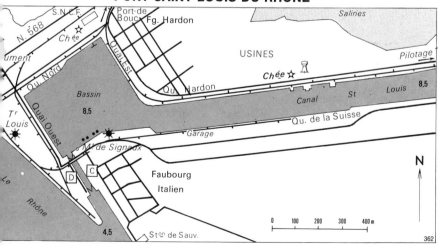

Route 13 **Messein to St. Jean-de-Losne**

Distance 275km
Number of locks 110
Minimum height above water 3,45m
Minimum depth of water 2,03m

	Kms	Locks		Michelin Map No.
CANAL DE L'EST			**MESSEIN**	62
		5		
	13		**CREVECHAMPS**	62
		10		
	19		**CHARMES**	62
		6		
	10		**NOMEXY**	62
		6		
	8		**THAON-LES-VOSGES**	62
(Left to Epinal) *RIGHT continue* *CANAL DE L'EST*	8		**EPINAL** (pop: 35 000). Noted for cotton weaving and lace making. Fine park on Castle Hill. Church: St. Maurice, 14thC. Museum: antiquities, pictures, and collection of Images d'Epinal.	62
		18		
	11		**CHAUMOUSEY**	62
		22		
	18		**THUNIMONT**	62
		6		
	6		**BAINS-LES-BAINS**	62
		9		
	10		**MONTMOTIER**	62
		3		
	6		**SELLES**	62
		6		
	11		**CORRE**	62,66
RIVER SAONE				
	3		**ORMOY**	66
		2		
	16		**MONTUREUX-LES-BAULAY**	66
		2		
	10		**CONFLANDEY**	66
	8		**PORT-SUR SAONE**	66
		4		
	11		**CHANTES**	66

	Kms	Locks	Route 13	Michelin Map No.
RIVER SAONE		3		
	13		**RAY-SUR-SAONE**	66
	10		**SAVOYEAUX**	66
		4		
	26		**GRAY** (pop: 8000). Market town in pretty setting. 15thC church. 16thC town hall.	66
		1		
	24		**HEUILLEY-SUR-SAONE**	66
(Right Canal de la Marne à la Saône)	2			
		1		
	3		**PONTAILLER-SUR-SAONE**	66
		1		
	16		**AUXONNE**	66
		1		
	13		**ST. JEAN-DE-LOSNE**	66

Route 14 **Paris to Conde**

Distance	179km
Number of locks	15
Minimum height above water	3,79m
Minimum depth of water	2,18m

	Kms	Locks		Michelin Map No.
RIVER SEINE To— *after PONT DE* *CONFLANS and just* *before PONT D'IVRY-S-* *SEINE. Turn LEFT into* *RIVER MARNE* *TUNNEL*	3		**PARIS**	56
		2		
	2		**JOINVILLE**	56
		2		
	23		**LAGNY**	56
	6			
TUNNEL				
		1		
(Right Canal de Meaux *à Chalifert)*	11		**MEAUX.** Market town, capital of the Brie. Episcopal palace, 12th–17thC. Bossuet museum.	56
	11		**GERMIGNY L'EVEQUE**	56
		1		
	11		**MARY-SUR-MARNE**	56
		1		
	11		**ST. JEAN-LES-DEUX-JUMEAUX**	56
	8		**LA FERTE**	56
		1		
	13		**SAACY**	56
		2		
	10		**CHARLY**	56
		1		
	10		**AZY**	56
	6		**CHATEAU-THIERRY** (pop: 11 000). Named after the castle built for King Thierry IV. Saw much action in both world wars. Nearby American National Cemetery of Bois-Belleau.	56

	Kms	Locks	Route 14	Michelin Map No.
RIVER MARNE			Situated amidst wooded countryside. La Fontaine born here.	
		I		
	10		**MONT-ST.-PERE**	56
		I		
	13		**DORMANS.** Pretty little market town.	56
		I		
	13		**PORT A BINSON**	56
		I		
	11		**CUMIERES**	56
(Junction to Epernay)			**EPERNAY** (pop: 25 000). Main centre for the production and export of champagne. The miles of cellars and Champagne Museum, Musée du Vin de Champagne in Château Perrier, Avenue de Champagne, are well worth a visit. Pleasant town, Haut-villers Abbey known as the 'cradle of champagne' because it was here that Dom Pérignon first perfected the making of champagne. There is a memorial to him in the abbey ruins. The following champagne cellars can be visited: Moët et Chandon, Mercier (guided tour in model railway), De Castellane, G. H. Martel, Perrier-Jouet, Pol Roger. Wine tasting. Details from *Syndicat d'Initiative*.	56
	2		**AY.** Possesses long historic links with wine making including a half-timbered building known as Henri IV's wine press. The following champagne cellars can be visited: Ayala, 2 Boulevard du Nord (Mon–Fri.); Bollinger, 16 Rue Jules Lobert (Mon–Fri., except August).	56
	5		**CONDE-SUR-MARNE**	56

Route 15 **Paris to St. Mammes**

Distance	82km
Number of locks	9
Minimum height above water	5,79m
Minimum depth of water	1,98m

	Kms	Locks		Michelin Map No.
RIVER SEINE			**PARIS**	61
		1		
	11		**VILLENEUVE ST. GEORGES** (Orly airport on RIGHT.)	61
		2		
	18		**CORBEIL**	61
		3		
	26		**MELUN** (pop: 27 000). Capital of Seine et Marne; by the Forest of Fontainebleu. Notre-Dame church, 11thC.	61
		3		
	27		**ST. MAMMES.** Junction for barge traffic.	61

48.   St. Mammes. Left, The Seine. Right, Canal du Loing.

Route 16 St. Mammes to Châlon-sur-Saône

Distance	395km
Number of locks	144
Minimum height above water	3,66m
Minimum depth of water	1,96m

	Kms	Locks		Michelin Map No.
CANAL DU LOING			**ST. MAMMES**	61
		2		
	2		**MORET-SUR-LOING.** Small town. Pleasant old houses.	61
		7		
	19		**NEMOURS.** Pleasant town in wooded setting. Museum.	61
		2		
	6		**GLANDELLES**	61
		1		
	3		**SOUPPES-SUR-LOING**	61
		4		
	10		**NARGIS**	61
		3		
	6		**CEPOY**	61
		1		
(Right Canal d'Orléans)	3		**BUGES**	61
RAIGHT ON CANAL		4		
DE BRIARE	5		**MONTARGIS** (pop: 17 000). Picturesque old town. Good fishing area. Madeleine Church, 12thC.	61,65
		6		
	11		**MONTCRESSON**	65
		1		
	6		**MONTBOUY**	65
		2		
	6		**CHATILLON-COLIGNY**	65
		5		
	10		**ROGNY**	65
		12		
	11		**OUZOUER-SUR-TREZEE**	65
CANAL LATERAL A LA LOIRE	5		**BRIARE** (pop: 4000). Small town. Principal claim to fame is the Pont Canal, 640m long, built by Eiffel in 1890 to carry the Briare Canal over the River Loire.	65

	Kms	Locks	Route 16	Michelin Map No.
CANAL LATERAL A LA LOIRE	8		**CHATILLON-SUR-LOIRE**	65
	6		**BEAULIEU**	65
		2		
	10		**LERE**	65
		3		
	11		**BANNAY**	65
	5		**SANCERRE** (pop: 3000). Wine region. Noted for Sancerre, Pouilly-Fumé, Menetou-Salon, Pouilly-Sur-Loire, and the V.D.Q.S. St. Pourcain-Sur-Sioule. Tasting at Cave Cooperative, Avenue de Verdun.	65
		3		
	13		**HERRY**	65
		4		
	13		**BEFFES**	65,69
(Right Canal du Berry)	3			
		4		
	13		**GUETIN**	69
		1		
	8		**PLAGNY**	69
	2		**NEVERS** (pop: 41 000). An interesting old town with medieval streets, chief town of the department of Nievre. Well known for pottery, the oldest of the earthenware factories was founded in 1648. Cathedral of St. Cyr, 11thC; St. Etienne church, 11thC; Ducal Palace, 15thC. Chapel of St. Gildard's Convent contains the body of St. Bernadette of Lourdes who died at Nevers in 1879. Museum with typical specimens of French and other faiences, also valuable assortment of enamels.	69
		1		
	11		**CHEVENON**	69
		4		
(Left junction to Decize)	21			
			DECIZE	69
		4		
	19		**GARNAT-SUR-ENGIEVRE**	69
		4		
	13		**DIOU**	69
		3		
	11		**COULANGES**	69

Kms	Locks	Route 16	Michelin Map No.
(Right Canal de Roanne à Digoin) 8	I		
ANAL DU CENTRE 3	I	**DIGOIN** (pop: 8000). Industrial town, well known for pottery. Pont-Canal with eleven arches connects Canal Latéral à la Loire with Canal du Centre.	69
11	3	**PARAY-LE-MONIAL**	69
16	5	**PALINGES**	69
21	8	**MONTCEAU-LES-MINES** (pop: 30 000). Mining town. Nearby Le Creusot is the centre of coalfields and heavy industry.	69
13	9	**MONTCHANIN**	69
13	15	**ST. BERAIN-SUR-DHEUNE**	69
10	6	**ST. GILLES**	69
3		**SANTENAY**	69
6	I	**CHAGNY** (pop: 5000). Thriving town between River Dheune and the canal. There are many of the famous Burgundy vineyards nearby: Chassagne-Mont-Rachet, Puligny-Montrachet, Meursault (tasting at La Maison de Meursault), Monthélie (tasting at Caves de Monthélie), Volnay (tasting at Caveau de Monsieur Boillot), Pommard. Beaune, 16km away and one of the most famous wine growing centres, is well worth a visit.	69
21	12	**CHALON-SUR-SAONE** (pop: 46 000). Inland port and naval dockyard. Industrial and commercial town; canal boats built here. Centre of wine-growing district of Burgundy, the Côte Chalonnaise producing rich, fragrant red wines (Mercurey, Givry) and the fresh, clear whites (Rully, Montagny). Fine old houses.	69

Route 17 St. Mammes to St. Jean-de-Losne

Distance	332km
Number of locks	209
Minimum height above water	3,38m
Minimum depth of water	1,96m

	Kms	Locks		Michelin Map No.
RIVER SEINE			**ST. MAMMES**	61
		1		
RIGHT into RIVER YONNE	13		**MONTEREAU** (pop: 10 000). Industrial town.	61
		6		
	32		**PONT-SUR-YONNE** (pop: 2000). Pleasant small town. Old bridge and historical remains. 12thC Church.	61
		2		
	11		**SENS** (pop: 21 000). Old town with cathedral begun in 1140, one of the greatest Gothic buildings, magnificent stained-glass windows, treasury collection among the best known in Europe; lapidary museum in 13thC Synodal Palace. The Cathedral of St. Etienne has relics of Thomas à Becket and his liturgical vestments.	61
		4		
	19		**VILLENEUVE-SUR-YONNE.** Interesting town. Old Royal residence.	61
		3		
	18		**JOIGNY** (pop: 8000). A pleasant little town, well known for its wine. Winding streets with half-timbered houses of 13th, 15th and 16thC. The arched bridge is 18thC. Riverside promenade. Churches: St. Thibault, 15thC; St. André, 11thC.	61,65
LEFT into CANAL DE BOURGOGNE	6	2	**LAROCHE.** Small town. Railway centre.	65
		5		
	18		**ST. FLORENTIN** (pop: 5000). Interesting little town, popular for fishing holidays. Noted for special cheese.	65
		7		
	13		**FLOGNY**	65
		4		
	13		**TONNERE** (pop: 5500). Old town. Wine centre. 13thC hospital with arched wooden roof contains	65

CANAL DE BOURGOGNE	Kms	Locks	Route 17	Michelin Map No.
			15thC Holy Sepulchre, one of the best Burgundian statues to survive. Notre-Dame Church, 13thC.	
		11		
	16		**ANCY-LE-LIBRE**	65
		10		
	21		**RAVIERES**	65
		11		
	19		**MONTBARD** (pop: 6000). Industrial town in pretty setting. The celebrated naturalist, Buffon, was born in Montbard and it was here that he wrote his *Natural History*; near the ruined castle is the Parc de Buffon.	65
		9		
	13		**VENAREY.** Nearby Château de Bussy with interesting portraits.	65
		10		
	3		**POUILLENAY**	65
		20		
	6		**MARIGNY-LE-CAHOUET**	65
		11		
	8		**BRAUX**	65
		2		
	10		**BEURIZOT**	65
		12		
	11		**POUILLY-EN-AUXOIS** (pop: 1000). Small town by the Canal Tunnel. Notre-Dame Church, 14thC.	65
TUNNEL		16		
	13		**CRUGEY**	65
		16		
	16		**GISSEY-SUR-OUCHE**	65,66
		13		
	13		**VERLARS-SUR-OUCHE**	65,66
		9		
	11		**DIJON** (pop: 140'000). Old medieval, industrial and wine trading city. Flourishing commercial and art centre. Many reminders that in the 15thC Dijon was a chief centre of European civilization. Cathedral: St. Benigne, 13thC. Church of Notre-Dame with celebrated Jack-o-the-clock. Palais de Justice, former seat of the Burgundy Parlement. Fine arts museum houses one of the oldest and best art galleries in France. Several other museums, Fragonard, Latour, Manet. From Dijon to Santenay (near to Chagny), is the Côte d'Or, the biggest wine-producing district of Burgundy. In the 24km from Dijon to Nuits St.	65,66

	Kms	*Locks*	**Route 17**	*Michelin Map No.*
CANAL DE BOURGOGNE			George are the estates of Marsanny-La-Cote, Gevrey-Chambertin (tasting in 17thC vaulted cellars of Maison Thomas Bassot), Chambolle-Musigny, Clos De Vougeot, Vosnee-Romanée.	
	6	7	**OUGES**	65,66
	10	8	**LONGECOURT-EN-PLANE**	65,66
	13	7	**ST. JEAN-DE-LOSNE.** Important in view of its position as a waterway junction of the Doubs and Saône rivers and the Burgundy, Centre and Rhône-Rhine canals.	

49.   St. Jean-de-Losne. Lock and basin beyond. The barge has ju
entered from the Saône.

Route 18 St. Nazaire to St. Malo

Route A to Redon

Distance	109km TO REDON
Number of locks	5
Minimum height above water	3,66m
Minimum depth of water	1,52m

Route B to Redon (coastal passage to the River Vilaine)

Distance (from La Roche Bernard)	39km TO REDON
Number of locks	1
Minimum depth of water	1,22m

ROUTE A to REDON

	Kms	Locks		Michelin Map No.
RIVER LOIRE			**ST. NAZAIRE** (pop: 60 000). Commercial and shipbuilding town with dockyards and harbour prominent. Greatly damaged during World War II, much of it by the Royal Navy attacking the German U-boat base. (See map on page 162.)	67
	8		**PAIMBOEUF**	67
	32		**NANTES** (pop: 250 000). Modern industrial town and commercial seaport. Chief claim to fame, the Edict of Nantes issued by Henry IV of France granting Protestants liberty of worship and equal political rights with Roman Catholics. Ducal Château, 14thC (in which Edict was signed). Museums: fine arts, archaeology, art, history of Nantes, and marine history of Nantes. Cathedral: St. Pierre, 15thC. Le Corbusier's new housing estate (Cité Radieuse) is just across the river at Rezé-les-Nantes. The vineyards of the Loire Valley are divided into four separate areas. Nearest to the sea are the wines of the region of Nantes. Then Anjou and Saumur and, further inland, Touraine and Sancerre. Muscadet is produced in the Nantes region, a light white wine, very fruity. Wine tasting at Caveau de Nantes, 17 Rue des Etats.	67
urn LEFT into RIVER ERDRE	13		**SUCE**	63
rn LEFT into CANAL NANTES A BREST	6			

	Kms	Locks	Route 18	Michelin Map No.
ANAL DE NANTES A BREST	13		**LA CHEVALLERAIS**	63
		3		
	6		**BLAIN**	63
		1		
	13		**GUENROUET**	63
		1		
	18		**REDON** (pop: 14 000). Small market town with some industry. Because of the silting of the River Vilaine, Redon has been cut off from the sea and port activity has decreased. The construction of a maritime lock at Arzal and the dredging of the bed of the Vilaine will enable marine traffic to use the port of Redon again. Church: St. Sauveur, 12thC.	63

ROUTE B to REDON

From St. Nazaire coastal passage 36km to River Vilaine, (see Admiralty Chart No. 2353).

	Kms	Locks		Michelin Map No.
RIVER VILAINE			**LA ROCHE BERNARD**	63
		1		
ANAL DE NANTES A BREST	29			
	10		**REDON** (by this route a mast need not be unstepped until Redon).	63

REDON to ST. MALO

Distance	184km
Number of locks	57
Minimum height above water	2,26m
Minimum depth of water	1,22m

	Kms	Locks		Michelin Map No.
Turn RIGHT into RIVER VILAINE			**REDON**	63
		2		
	21		**MESSAC**	63
		1		
	8		**ST. MALO-DE-PHILY**	63
		4		

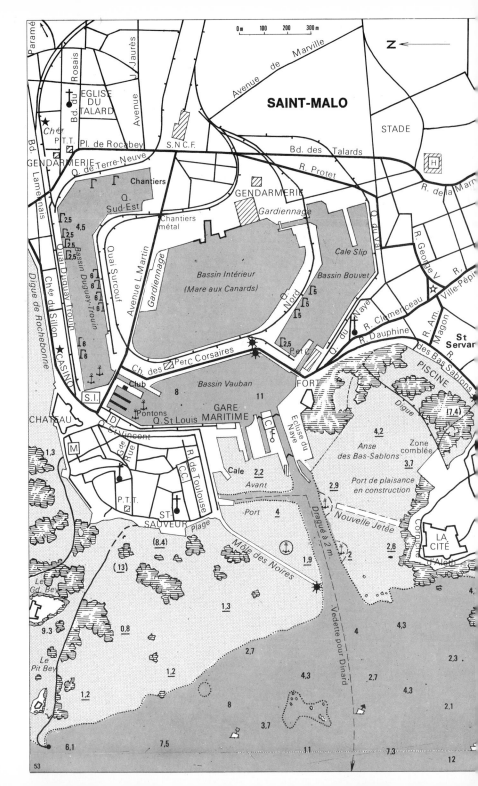

SAINT-MALO

Paramé

Bd. du Rosais

Avenue de Marville

Z ←

EGLISE DU TALARD

Avenue J. Jaurès

STADE

Chée P.T.T.

Pl. de Rocabey

S.N.C.F.

Bd. des Talards

H

GENDARMERIE

Q. de Terre-Neuve

R. Protet

R. de la Mari

Bd. Lamennais

Chantiers

GENDARMERIE

Digue de Rochebonne

Q. Sud-Est

Chantiers métal

Gardiennage

Cale Slip

R. George V

R. des Bas-Sablons

R. Am. Magon

R. Ville-Pépir

St Servar

2,5 4,5
2,5
2,5
2,5

Quai Surcouf

Avenue L. Martin

Gardiennage

Bassin Intérieur
(Mare aux Canards)

Bassin Bouvet

Q. du Val

6
6

Q. Nord

5
5
5

2,5

Q. de la Nave

R. Clémenceau
R. Dauphine

Bassin Duguay-Trouin

Quai Duguay-Trouin

CASINO

6
6

Petc C

PISCIE

S.I.

Ch. des Petc Corsaires

FORT

Digue

(17,4)

CHATEAU

Club

Pontons

8

Bassin Vauban

11

GARE MARITIME

Écluse du Nave

4,2

Anse des Bas-Sablons

Zone comblée

3,7

1,3

M

Q. St Vincent

Q. St Louis

C

Port de plaisance en construction

2,9

P.T.T.

G. de Rue

R. de Toulouse

C.C.I.

Cale

2,2

Avant

2,6

LA CITÉ

ST-SAUVEUR

plage

-Port 4

Môle des Noires

1,9

Nouvelle Jetée

d'Aleth

2

(8,4)

Dragué à 2 m

(13)

Le Gd. Bey

1,3

4,3

4,

9,3

0,8

2,7

4

Le Pit Bey

1,2

4,3

2,7

2,3 .

1,2

8

4,3

2,1

3,7

6,1

7,5

1,1

7,3

12

53

Kms	Locks	Route 18	Michelin Map No.
21		**PONT REAN**	63
	5		
18		**RENNES** (pop: 190 000). Industrial and agricultural centre. Capital of the department of Ile-et-Vilaine. Palais de Justice, 17thC. Cathedral, 19thC. Museum: Latour, Poussin.	63,59
	3		
6		**ST. GREGOIRE**	59
	3		
10		**BETTON**	59
	5		
13		**ST. GERMAIN-SUR-ILLE**	59
	6		
10		**MONTREUIL-SUR-ILLE**	59
	13		
16		**TINTENIAC**	59
	7		
13		**TREVERIEN**	59
	2		
6		**EVRAN**	59
	5		
11		**DINAN** (pop: 18 000). Old walled town. Quaint streets and picturesque houses. 14thC castle. Church: St. Sauveur, 14thC.	59
	1		
		LA VICOMTE	59
31		**ST. MALO** (pop: 19 000). Attractive and historic seaport; with its town walls it still resembles a medieval fortress. Derives its name from a Welsh monk. Much damaged in World War II and rebuilt on original lines. Castle: 14thC. Church: St. Vincent, 13thC.	59

Left margin notes:

RIVER VILAINE (beside RENNES)

rn LEFT into CANAL D'ILLE ET RANCE

RIVER RANCE (beside LA VICOMTE)

Route 19 St. Valéry to St. Simon

Distance	156km
Number of locks	26
Minimum height above water	3,45m
Minimum depth of water	1,70m

	Kms	Locks		Michelin Map No.
CANAL DE LA SOMME			**ST. VALERY-SUR-SOMME** (pop: 3000). Pleasantly situated little holiday resort.	52
		2		
	16		**ABBEVILLE** (pop: 23 000). Largely rebuilt following air raids of World War II. Belonged to England for 200 years from 1272 on marriage of Edward I to Eleanor of Castile. Museum: ceramics, paintings; collection of wild fowl of the Somme valley.	52
		1		
	10		**PONT-REMY**	52
		3		
	23		**PICQUIGNY**	52,53
		3		
	16		**AMIENS** (pop: 120 000). Ancient capital of Picardy, now of the department of Somme. Headquarters of the British Army in World War I. Largely destroyed in World War II and rebuilt on modern lines. World famous textile centre for manufacture of velvet. Cathedral of Notre-Dame is the largest in France (completed 1269) and one of the greatest architectural creations in the world. Museum: rich collection of paintings, Bonnard, Fragonard, Gaugin, Matisse. Water market of boats selling fruit and vegetables.	52,53
		2		
	13		**DAOURS**	52,53
		1		
	5		**CORBIE**	52,53
		1		
	11		**CHIPILLY**	52,53
		5		
	19		**FRISE**	52,53
		1		
	10		**PERONNE** (pop: 7000). Almost completely rebuilt following war damage; featured in the	52,53

Kms	Locks	Route 19	Michelin Map No.
CANAL DE LA SOMME		Battle of the Somme. Two museums. Church: St. John, 1520.	
8	1	**ST. CHRIST**	52,53
5	1	**PARGNY**	52,53
8		**VOYENNES**	52,53
6	3	**HAM**	53
6	2	**ST. SIMON**	53

Route 20 Strasbourg to Châlon-sur-Saône

Distance	377km
Number of locks	151
Minimum height above water	3,48m
Minimum depth of water	1,98m

	Kms	Locks		Michelin Map No.
CANAL DU RHONE			**STRASBOURG**	87
AU RHIN		5		
	11		**ESCHAU**	87
		11		
	27		**SUNDHOUSE**	87
		5		
	11		**MARCKOLSHEIM**	87
(Right to Colmar)				

To the west of the Canal du Rhône au Rhin, from Strasbourg to Mulhouse, are 45 000 acres of vineyards dating back to Roman times. La Route du Vin d'Alsace is, in fact, from Wangen to Thann, and the most convenient point near the waterway from which to visit this wine area is COLMAR. Among the great wines to have made Alsace famous are Sylvaner, Riesling, Pinot Blanc, Gewürz-Traminer, Tokay, the Muscatels, and Zwicker.

	Kms		Michelin Map No.
	6	**COLMAR** (pop: 62 000). One of the most attractive old towns in Alsace. Many fine old wooden houses of the 16th–17thC. Cathedral: 13thC; Dominican's church: 13thC. Wine capital of Alsace, retaining the aspect of an old Alsatian town. The Unterlinden museum contains a reconstructed Alsatian wine cellar and wine museum, also the Isenheim altarpiece by Mathias Grünewald, one of the world's greatest paintings. From Colmar there are coach excursions to La Route du Vin d'Alsace.	87
CANAL DU RHONE	2		
AU RHIN 3		**KUNHEIM**	87
(Left to Briesach, German frontier)			
	3		
	6	**NEUF-BRISACH**	87

	Kms	Locks	Route 20	Michelin Map No.
CANAL DU RHONE		13		
AU RHIN	23		**MUNCHHOUSE**	87,66
		5		
(Left Canal de Huningue	13		**MULHOUSE** (pop: 120 000). Industrial town, largest in the Upper Rhine Department; spinning and weaving. Was German town for fifty years up to 1918. Town Hall built in 1552; Chapel of St. Jean, former possession of the Knights of Malta. Museum of weaving and textiles. Large zoo.	87,66
to Swiss frontier)				
		6		
	6		**ZILLISHEIM**	87,66
		8		
	11		**HAGENBACH**	87,66
		14		
	11		**MONTREUX**	87,66
		4		
	10		**FROIDEFONTAINE**	87,66
		8		
	13		**MONTBELIARD** (pop: 20 000). Industrial town. 18thC Château des Princes, now a museum, overlooks the town. Quaint old houses.	87,66
		7		
	11		**COLOMBIER-FONTAINE**	66
		6		
	13		**L'ISLE-SUR-LE-DOUBS**	66
		6		
	13		**CLERVAL**	66
		7		
	16		**BAUME-LES-DAMES** (pop: 5000). Ancient	66

50.   Between Clerval and Baume-les-Dames.

	Kms	Locks	Route 20	Michelin Map No.
CANAL DU RHONE AU RHIN			town, named after a nunnery that was once on the site. Many 18thC houses.	
		5		
	13		**LAISSEY**	66
		4		
	21		**BESANCON** (pop: 100 000). Important town, centre of the French watchmaking industry, also artificial silk. Palais de Justice, 16thC; once meeting place of the Franche-Comté. Birthplace of Victor Hugo, also Lumière brothers, inventors of the moving picture. Museum contains interesting watch and clock section. Many gracious buildings.	66
		4		
TUNNEL	11		**THORAISE**	66
		5		
	16		**FRAISANS**	66
		9		
	23		**DOLE** (pop: 28 000). Old town, ancient capital of Franche-Comté. Rich in history and architecture of 16th, 17th, and 18thC. Five museums. The vineyards of ARBOIS, 30kms away to the East, are the first to be given *Appellation Contrôlée* by the French Government. The wines produced around Arbois, in the Jura foothills, are white, red, and rose. The great names of the Jura vineyards are Arbois, Etoile, Château Chalon, and Cotes Du Jura.	66,70
		9		
LEFT into RIVER SAONE	18		**ST. SYMPHORIEN** (pop: 2000).	70
(Right Canal du Bourgogne)	3		**ST. JEAN-DE-LOSNE**	70
		2		
	13		**LECHATELET**	70
		1		
	13		**SEURRE** (pop: 2000). Pleasant old town.	70
		2		
(From Left River Doubs)	16		**VERDUN-SUR-EL-DOUBS.** Restaurants offer fish speciality.	70
(From Right Canal de Centre)	24			
		2		
			CHALON-SUR-SAONE	70

Route 21 **Toul to Strasbourg**

via FROUARD

Distance	181km
Number of locks	80
Minimum height above water	3,68m
Minimum depth of water	2,18m

	Kms	Locks		Michelin Map No.
CANAL DE LA			**TOUL**	62
MARNE AU RHIN		3		
	16		**LIVERDUN.** Attractive medieval town.	62
TUNNEL				
		1		
(Left River Moselle to	6		**FROUARD.** Town of heavy industry.	62
Metz and Luxembourg/				
Germany)	10		**NANCY** (pop: 150 000). Capital of Lorraine in the heart of an important industrial region. Old university town. Fine example of baroque town planning, much of which remains. Magnificent public squares, largest, Place Stanislas, surrounded by palaces. Ducal Palace: 16thC. Five museums with Delacroix, Manet.	62
		1		
(Right Canal de l'Est)	6		**LANEUVILLE-DEVANT-NANCY**	62
		2		
	11		**VARANGEVILLE**	62
		6		
	13		**EINVILLE**	62
		3		
	13		**XURES**	62
		6		
	11		**MOUSSEY**	62
(Left Canal des Houille				
de la Sarre to German				
frontier)		6		
	6		**GONDREXANGE**	62,87
	8		**HEMING**	62,87
	8		**HESSE**	87,62
TUNNEL	10			
	22			

	Kms	Locks	Route 21	Michelin Map No.
CANAL DE LA MARNE AU RHIN	10		**LUTZELBOURG**	87,62
		9		
	10		**SAVERNE**	87,62
		5		
	8		**DETTWILLER**	87
		7		
	13		**WALTENHEIM-S-ZORN**	87
		5		
	11		**VENDENHEIM**	87
		4		
	11		**STRASBOURG** (pop: 250 000). Capital of the	87

STRASBOURG (pop: 250 000). Capital of the department of Bas-Rhin. Important river port, commercial and cultural centre. Has belonged to France and Germany in turn, became French again in 1918. Both architectural influences are apparent. Much damaged in World War II. Cathedral Notre-Dame: 12thC. Famous clock. Museums: furniture, domestic, also Corot, Fragonard, Watteau, Dégas, Monet, Renoir, Braque, Gaugin.

51.   The inclined plane, St. Louis-Arzviller.   *Photo Karquel*

52. Chalons-sur-Marne. Canal latéral à la Marne.

Photo Yan

Route 22 **Vitry-le-François to Messein**

Distance   156km
Number of locks   98
Minimum height above water   3,68m
Minimum depth of water   2,18m

	Kms	Locks		Michelin Map No.
CANAL DE LA MARNE AU RHIN		4	VITRY-LE-FRANCOIS	61
	13		BIGNICOURT	61
	11	7	SERMAIZE-LES-BAINS	61
	13	13	MUSSEY	61,65
	8	7	BAR-LE-DUC (pop: 20 000). Industrial town, capital of the department of Meuse. Ancient houses. Church of St. Etienne containing gruesome statue: (the skeleton of Prince René de Châlons, whose dying wish was that his tomb effigy should resemble his body three years after his death). Monument to Pierre and Ernest Michaux who invented the pedal cycle.	61,62
	8	7	TANNOIS	62
	8	10	LIGNY-EN-BARROIS	62
	13	11	TREVERAY	62
	8	9	DEMANGE-AUX-EAUX	62
TUNNEL		1		
	10		MAUVAGES	62
	10	12	VOID	62
	10		TROUSSEY	62
TUNNEL	10	10		
	10		TOUL (pop: 14 000). Old fortified town. Tourist centre of Lorraine. Ancient ramparts and twin-	62

53. Toul. Canal de la Marne au Rhin.

	Kms	Locks	Route 22	Michelin Map No.
RIGHT into CANAL DE L'EST (Left to Sedan and Belgian frontier)			towered cathedral, 13thC. Church: St. Gengoult, 13thC. Joan of Arc once came to Toul. A young man from her village pretended that she had promised to marry him and indicted her before Henri de Ville, Bishop of Toul.	
		1		
	3		**CHAUDENAY-SUR-MOSELLE**	62
		4		
	19		**PONT ST. VINCENT**	62
		2		
	2		**MESSEIN**	62

Route 23 **Watten to Chauny**

Distance	240km
Number of locks	50
Minimum height above water	3,68m
Minimum depth of water	2,18m

	Kms	Locks		Michelin Map No.
RIVER AA			**WATTEN**	51
		1		
CANAL DE NEUFFOSSE	8		**ST. OMER** (pop: 20 000). Centre of Agriculture. Much damaged in both world wars. Notre-Dame, 13thC. Museum: fine arts, paintings include four of Breughel the Elder including the celebrated 'Surgical Operation'.	51
		6		
(Left Canal de la Nieppe to River Lys to Belgian frontier)	19	(or lift)	**AIRE-SUR-LA-LYS** (pop: 10 000). On the River Lys and Canal d'Aire, 17thC town.	51
CANAL D'AIRE				
(Right to Bethune)	21		**BETHUNE** (pop: 25 000). Industrial town with docks. Much damaged in both world wars. British cemetery of World War I at Neuve Chapelle, 9km away.	51,53
		2		
	13		**LA BASSEE**	51,53
n RIGHT into CANAL DE LA DEULE	6			
(Left to Lille and Belgian frontier)			**LILLE** (pop: 200 000). Big industrial town, one of the greatest textile centres in the world. Was once named l'Isle, thus Lisle thread which came from here. Birthplace of Général de Gaulle. Modern cathedral. Museum holds richest collection of art outside Paris with Goyas, Rubens, Franz Hals, Van Dyck, Veronese, Titian, Delacroix, Corot, Monet, Sisley, Renoir.	51,53
VAL DE LA DEULE	6		**BAUVIN**	51,53
	6		**VENDIN-LE-VIEIL**	51,53
(Right Canal de Lens to Lens)	11		**LENS** (pop: 42 000). An industrial town in a	51,53

	Kms	Locks	Route 23	Michelin Map No.
CANAL DE LA DEULE			mining area with long lines of slag heaps.	
(River Scarpe Left to Belgian frontier Right to Arras)	16			
DOUAI BY-PASS CANAL is main route			**DOUAI.** An important industrial centre in the heart of the coal basin.	51,53
CANAL DE LA SENSEE			**CORBEHEM**	53
		I		
(Right Canal du Nord)	10		**ARLEUX**	53
	13		**PAILLENCOURT**	53
Turn RIGHT into RIVER ESCAUT (Left to Belgian frontier)		4		
	11		**CAMBRAI** (pop: 36 000). Prosperous town noted for weaving and fine linen cloth; 'cambric' invented here. Saw much action in World War I, tanks first used in Battle of Cambrai, November 1917. Much damage which was restored, destroyed again in World War II and restored again.	53
CANAL DE SAINT-QUENTIN				
		4		
	6		**MARCOING**	53
		2		
	3		**MASNIERES**	53
		6		
	11		**BANTOUZELLE**	53
		3		
	3		**HONNECOURT-SUR-ESCAUT**	53
		2		
	3		**VENDHUILE**	53
TUNNEL				
	16		**LESDINS**	53
		3		
	6		**OMISSY**	53
		2		
	6		**ST. QUENTIN** (pop: 60 000). Industrial centre, textiles. Interesting town, rich in historical association. Fine Hôtel de Ville. Museum: works of Quentin de la Tour.	53
		I		
	8		**FONTAINE-LES-CLERCS**	53
		I		
	6		**ARTEMPS**	53
		I		
	2		**TUGNY-ET-PONT**	53

54.   Arras on the River Scarpe.   *Photo J. Feuillie*

	Kms	Locks	Route 23	Michelin Map No.
CANAL DE SAINT		1		
QUENTIN	2		**ST. SIMON**	53
(Right Canal de la				
Somme)				
	10		**JUSSY**	53
		2		
	5		**MENNESSIS**	53
		1		
	3		**QUESSY**	53,56
		3		
	2		**TERGNIER**	56
(Left to La Fère to join				
Canal de la Sambre à l'Oise				
to Landrecies and frontier)		4		
	8		**CHAUNY** (pop: 12 000). Industrial town.	56

55.   From the French canals it is easy to enter Belgian and Dutch waters
such as the River Ling at Gelderland.   *Photo L. Philippe*

From Belgium into France

Route BF/1 **Furnes to Dunkirk**

Distance	22km
Number of locks	1
Minimum height above water	3,50m
Minimum depth of water	1,80m
Maximum LOA	40,40m
Maximum beam	6m

	Kms	Locks		Michelin Map No.
CANAL DE NIEUW- *ORT A DUNKERQUE*		1	**FURNES**	
	4		**ADINKERKE.** The district is a place of pilgrimage to the many war cemeteries.	
			FRONTIER	
NTINUE AS CANAL *DE FURNES*	4		**BRAY-DUNES**	51
	6		**ZUYDCOOTE**	51
	7		**ROSENDAEL**	51
	1		**DUNKIRK**	51

Route BF/2 **Menin to Armentières**

Distance	51km
Number of locks	3
Minimum height above water	4m
Minimum depth of water	1,90m
Maximum LOA	42,32m
Maximum beam	5,40m

Kms Locks

RIVER LYS		**MENIN**	
	1		
	4	**WERVIK** (pop: 13 000).	
	7	**COMINES** (pop: 9000). Industrial town.	
	1		
	6	**WARNETON**	

From here the river is the frontier between Belgium and France
for 25km. Jointly owned.

			Michelin
	FRONTIER		*Map No.*
RIVER LYS	2	**DEULEMONT**	51
(Left Canal de la Deule)			
	2	**FRELINGHEIN**	51
	1		
	5	**ARMENTIERES**	51

Route BF/3 **Espierres to Lille**

Distance	32km
Number of locks	16
Minimum height above water	3,65m
Minimum depth of water	1,80m
Maximum LOA	38,43m
Maximum beam	5,14m

	Kms	Locks		Michelin Map No.
CANAL DE L'ESPIERRES			**ESPIERRES**	
		1		
	3		**ST. LEGER**	
		2		
	5		**LEERS-NORD**	
			FRONTIER	
CANAL DE ROUBAIX			**LEERS**	51
		4		
	5		**ROUBAIX**	51
		1		
	4		**TOURCOING**	51
		7		
	10			
LEFT into CANAL DE LA DEULE			**MARQUETTE**	51
		1		
	5		**LILLE**	51

Route BF/4 **Antoing to Douai**

Distance	52km
Number of locks	6
Minimum height above water	3,70m
Minimum depth of water	2,10m
Maximum LOA	38,50m
Maximum beam	5,15m

	Kms	*Locks*		*Michelin Map No.*
RIVER ESCAUT			**ANTOING**	
	6		**PERONNES**	
	4		**BLEHARIES**	
			FRONTIER	
Join (from Left) *RIVER SCARPE*	3	2	**MORTAGNE DU NORD**	51
	11		**ST. AMAND-LES-EAUX**	51
	9	2	**WARLAING**	51
	12	2	**LALLAING**	51
	7		**DOUAI**	51

Route BF/5 **Antoing to Conde**

Distance	26km
Number of locks	1
Minimum height above water	3,70m
Minimum depth of water	2,10m
Maximum LOA	38,50m
Maximum beam	5,15m

	Kms	*Locks*		*Michelin Map No.*
RIVER ESCAUT			**ANTOING**	
	6		**PERONNES**	
	4		**BLEHARIES**	
			FRONTIER	
RIVER ESCAUT	3		**MORTAGNE DU NORD**	51
		1		
	7		**HERGNIES**	51
	6		**CONDE-SUR-L'ESCAUT**	51

Route BF/6 **Blaton to Conde**

Distance	11km
Number of locks	8
Minimum height above water	3,70m
Minimum depth of water	1,80m
Maximum LOA	38,50m
Maximum beam	5,10m

	Kms	Locks		Michelin Map No.
CANAL DE POMMER-OEUL A ANTOING			**BLATON**	
(Junction Canal Nimy-Blaton)				
RIGHT into CANAL DE MONS A CONDE	5			
	8	1	**HENSIES**	
			FRONTIER	
CANAL DE MONS A CONDE		2	**ST. AYBERT**	51
	3		**CONDE**	51

Route BF/7 **Charleroi to Maubeuge**

Distance	52kms
Number of locks	13
Minimum height above water	3,25m
Minimum depth of water	1,90m
Maximum LOA	38,50m
Maximum beam	5,15m

	Kms	Locks		
RIVER SAMBRE			**CHARLEROI**	
(From Left Canal				
de Charleroi	2			
a Bruxelles)		2		
	5		**MONTIGNIES-LE-TILLEUL**	
		4		
	13		**THUIN.** Pleasantly situated above the Sambre. Interesting historical associations include the base of the Tour Notger, a relic of the fortifications set up by the Bishop of that name around 1000. Early 16thC abbey.	
		4		
	15		**MERBES-LE-CHATEAU**	
		1		
	5		**ERQUELINNES**	
				Michelin Map No.
			FRONTIER	
RIVER SAMBRE			**JEUMONT**	51
		2		
	12		**MAUBEUGE**	51

Route BF/8 **Namur to Pont-a-Bar**

Distance	143km
Number of locks	28
Minimum height above water	3,70m
Minimum depth of water	2,20m
Maximum LOA	48,30m
Maximum beam	5,70m

Kms Locks

RIVER MEUSE   **NAMUR**

         1

6   **WEPION.** Attractive holiday centre, famous for strawberries. Strawberries Sunday is the third in June.

         1

6   **PROFONDEVILLE.** Pleasant spot, but rather crowded at weekends during summer.

         1

5   **GODIN**

2   **YVOIR**

         1

5   **ANHEE**

         1

3   **BOUVIGNIES.** Pleasant little town with a number of old buildings well restored after destruction of World War I.

         1

2   **DINANT** (pop: 10 000). Main tourist centre for the Belgian Ardennes and holiday resort on the River Meuse, situated beneath an almost vertical cliff. Pleasant town with a long acquaintance with war and sackings; in 1944 the Americans drove the Nazis from the citadel. Largely rebuilt. 13thC Notre-Dame church, with bulbous Baroque tower, Citadel with museum. Telesiege of Dinant takes you by chairlift to the tower of the Mont-Fat, 110m above the River Meuse. *Syndicat d'Initiative*: Hôtel de Ville.

2   **ANSEREMME.** An attractive river resort.

         1

7   **WAULSORT**

         1

4   **HASTIERE-LAVAUX**

	Kms	Locks		Route BF/8	
RIVER MEUSE		I			
	5		**HEER**		
			FRONTIER		*Michelin Map No.*
		I		**GIVET**	53
TUNNEL	7	I	**CHOOZ**		53
	7	3	**VIREUX**		53
	6	I	**MONTIGNY-SUR-MEUSE**		53

56. Dinant.

Photo L. Philippe

	Kms	Locks	Route BF/8	Michelin Map No.
RIVER MEUSE		2		
	7		**FUMAY**	53
		3		
TUNNEL	12		**REVIN**	53
		3		
	11		**LAIFOUR**	53
		1		
	9		**MONTHERME**	53
		2		
	12		**NOUZONVILLE**	53
		1		
	9		**MEZIERES**	53
		1		
	6		**LUMES**	53
		1		
	9		**PONT-A-BAR**	53

From Germany and Luxembourg into France

route GLF/1 Remerschen to Frouard

Distance	105km
Number of locks	18
Minimum height above water	3,70m
Minimum depth of water	2,60m
Maximum LOA	39,60m
Maximum beam	6m

The Moselle forms the frontier between Germany and the Grand Duchy of Luxembourg.

	Kms	Locks		
RIVER MOSELLE			**REMERSCHEN**	
	2			*Michelin*
	FRONTIER		RIGHT BANK: Grand Duchy of Luxembourg	*Map No.*
			LEFT BANK: Germany	
	2		**CONTZ-LES-BAINS**	57
	7		**MALLING**	57
		1		
	14		**THIONVILLE** (pop: 26 000).	57
		2		
	14		**TALANGE**	57
		2		
	15		**METZ** (pop: 150 000). Ancient Gallic town that was fortified by the Romans.	57
		3		
JUNCTION	12		**ANCY-SUR-MOSELLE**	57
	4		**CORNY-SUR-MOSELLE**	57
		3		
	6		**PAGNY-SUR-MOSELLE**	57
		1		
	6		**PONT-A-MOUSSON**	57
		2		
	10		**DIEULOUARD**	57
		1		
	9		**MARBACHE**	57
		3		
	4		**FROUARD**	57

Note: On many German waterways the skipper of a motor cruiser/yacht must be in possession of an official 'Driver's Licence'.

From Germany into France

Route GF/2 **Kleinblittersdorf to Gondrexange**

Distance	73km
Number of locks	27
Minimum height above water	3,65m
Minimum depth of water	2,20m
Maximum LOA	39m
Maximum beam	5,20m

	Kms	Locks		Michelin Map No.
RIVER SAAR			**KLEINBLITTERSDORF**	
			FRONTIER	
CANAL DES	11		**SARREGUEMINES**	57
HOUILLERES DE		5		
LA SARRE	11		**WITTRING**	57
		3		
	11		**SARRALBE**	57
		4		
	12		**HARSKIRCHEN**	57
		2		
	9		**MITTERSHEIM**	57
		13		
	19		**GONDREXANGE**	57

Route GF/3 **Lauterbourg to Strasbourg**

Distance	61km
Number of locks	1
Minimum height above water	7m
Minimum depth of water	2,70m
Maximum LOA	185m
Maximum beam	23m

	Kms	Locks		Michelin Map No.
RIVER RHINE			**LAUTERBOURG**	87
	21		**SELTZ**	87
	20		**DRUSENHEIM**	87
	20	1	**STRASBOURG**	87

The Rhine forms the frontier between France and Germany for 200km, from the Swiss frontier at Basle to Lauterbourg.

From Basle south into France, the Canal de Huningue links (from Niffer to Mulhouse), with the Canal du Rhône au Rhin (see Route 20).

ndex

The Harbour Plans are supplied by
EDITIONS MARITIMES ET
D'OUTRE-MER who are publishers of
the RENAULT MARINE GUIDE. This
contains Harbour Plans of every harbour in
France, plus much information of value to
the yachtsman. They also publish Strip
Maps of the French Waterways. Details
may be obtained from EDITIONS
MARITIMES ET D'OUTRE-MER,
17, Rue Jacob, PARIS-6.